HX

GHOSTS

GHOSTS OF TARGETS PAST

PHILIP GRAY

Edited by E. J. Coulter

ISIS
LARGE PRINT
Oxford

First published in Great Britain 2005
by
Grub Street

Published in Large Print 2009 by ISIS Publishing Ltd.,
7 Centremead, Osney Mead, Oxford OX2 0ES
by arrangement with
Grub Street

British Library Cataloguing in Publication Data
Gray, Philip.
    Ghosts of targets past the lives and losses of a
    Lancaster crew in 1944–1945. - - (Reminiscence)
    1. Gray, Philip.
    2. World War, 1939–1945 - - Aerial operations,
    British.
    3. World War, 1939–1945 - - Personal narratives,
    British.
    4. Lancaster (Bombers)
    5. Large type books.
    I. Title II. Series
    940.5'44'941'092–dc22

ISBN 978–0–7531–9542–0 (hb)
ISBN 978–0–7531–9543–7 (pb)

Printed and bound in Great Britain by
T. J. International Ltd., Padstow, Cornwall

This book is dedicated to the memory of Arthur "Ginger" Lewis, who died "in action" while still trying to earn that coveted wings brevet. At twenty-one years of age, his life was barely into second gear. He now lies at rest for ever in a small cemetery plot in the Arizona desert. Indeed, such a dedication must include all aircrew who paid the ultimate price during the holocaust of World War Two.

Contents

Prologue

We were about to kill a town!

Now, there was something we had never done before. Indeed, until three hours back, none of us had ever heard of this place called Wesel. It was situated on the east side of the Rhine, no doubt picturesque and appealing, its only crime being that of location. It was in the way.

As a bomber crew, pounding along at 19,500 feet toward an enemy target, my friends and I were about to have the ultimate choice punched straight at us: kill or be killed? There is always this choice, of course: either stand to and fight, or cut loose and run for cover. This was our maiden operational flight, the first time we had flown up to the sharp end of a war.

The German army had dug in on the Wesel side of the famous European waterway, while the Allied armies in this area, under the leadership of Field Marshal Montgomery, were stamping impatiently on the west side. Such a classic stand-off was a sitter for the equally classic solution: send in Bomber Command to soften things up a bit. Truly, background was of little immediate importance to those in the bomber stream.

To the seven in our Lancaster R-Roger, valiantly trying to hold up our end of the attack, survival was the only issue.

Fear of the unknown was churning the contents of our bowels to water, all our knowledge and information about aerial warfare being hearsay and secondhand.

There were 370 bombers zeroing in on the target in one continuous stream, our R-Roger flying about a third of the way back from the lead plane.

Just ten minutes to go now. Pock-mark bursts of spent and exploding anti-aircraft shells were clearly visible. They looked horrific hanging there in the gloriously blue sky. We had never seen such organised bedlam before.

"You watching the flak, Skip?" The question from the Mid-upper Gunner found a gap in the radio intercom.

"I'm watching it, Blondie," I replied, missing out the last part of the sentence which would have added something like, "and it's doing the same to me as it's doing to you. It's got me shitting blue lights."

Other messages passed over the intercom network inside the plane, most of them relevant to the work at hand. The Rear Gunner warned that one of our planes following behind was beginning to drift forward and above us. Bomb Aimer and Navigator exchanged notes and instructions, readying for the release of our bombs and incendiaries.

But the flak was the big issue. It was burning a hole in Blondie's thoughts and, now about five miles short of the luckless town, his voice squeezed in again through the rest of the chatter.

"They say that females are in charge of most German anti-aircraft batteries. Each babe controls four guns from a radar screen," he informed.

"I've heard that, too," came a chip-in from the Rear Gunner.

"In that case, Skip," Blondie bounced back (and this was the bit that had been niggling him all along), "have you noticed that witch creeping up on our port side? She's coming along real well. Any closer and she could cancel our tickets."

"Believe me," I said, sounding as soothing as I could in the circumstances, "she hasn't passed unnoticed but she's got our ass in a bucket. There's frig all I can do about it."

"But if sh . . . ," started the Mid-upper again.

"Sorry, Blondie," I cut in, "but we're getting too close. Let's leave the air free for Gerry and Jack. They've got things to organise."

"Ah yes . . . sorry."

No need to be all that sorry, my friend. I just didn't want to hear any more. In the middle of the maintenance flying — keeping the airspeed, height, and direction as called for; bouncing and bucking in the "backwash" of the aircraft further up the stream; scudding in and out of the artificial clouds coming off other wingtips — in the middle of all of this, yes, I too had noticed that particular line of flak.

About the ten-mile point, the first bracket of four explosions had appeared way out to port, and well ahead. True, lots of other quartets of exploding shells were being registered, some above our flight line and some below, but there was something ominous about this lot. If there was a maiden in charge of the trigger down there, then she certainly knew her business.

These explosions were right on our height, each successive salvo moving closer, each one neatly spaced out. As Blondie was about to suggest when I cut him short, if this lady maintained her form, and we certainly had no alternative at all but to rigidly hold our preplanned ride in on target, then the next salvo and our Lancaster were flush on a collision course! Reality called the shots. There was no place to hide.

Mercifully, a request from the Bomb Aimer cut through the agony like a bucket of iced water.

"Bomb doors open, Phil."

I nodded to the Engineer, and he plunged the lever down.

"Bomb doors open," I came back, watching the indicator click at the end of its run down the gauge.

From now on the Bomb Aimer expected precision flying. Course, airspeed and height had to be frozen exactly as they were. Any careless twist of the control column now and the bombs would veer far off target. Other diversions were erupting ahead. I could see 500-pounders falling away in precise groupings from other bombers. In stark contrast, 4,000-pound "Cookies" somersaulted almost playfully as they started their lethal plunge earthwards.

"Over on the starboard side, Skip, I think Sugar's been hit," informed Clin from the rear turret.

"Keep checking, Clin," I said, "but keep the air free for Jack."

In the build-up of the carnage over the target, no one had noticed the minor miracle. That expected, final lethal salvo of flak never came. Either the gun controller had changed her tactics or "somebody up there" really was on our side.

Jack's instructions now monopolized the intercom.

"About two degrees to port, Phil." "Starboard a little." "A little more." "Back port a shade." "Shade more port." "Steady at that." "Steady." "Steady."

Right over the target, bombers were drifting in all directions, possibly engaged in the same caper as ourselves. Our Lancaster suddenly reared in relief as our cargo fell away from its holders, confirmation coming from the Bomb Aimer.

"Bombs away!"

The bomb doors slammed shut as fast as the Engineer could hit the lever. We could no longer be diced up into little pieces if a stray piece of shrapnel sliced into our gaping bomb bay. This relief and the jockeying for survival pushed us through to the other side of the target in a blur. The fear, the explosions, the fate of the other bombers had all happened so fast that this first operational adventure was over before we could fully understand what was unreeling before us. With practice we would begin to see the whole picture, all the horrifying detail. Perhaps we should have done only the one operational flight!

The long, gradual let-down to safety had blissfully begun. No drink ever before, or after, could match the flavour of the coffee from our flasks at this time. It tasted like liquid gold.

5

Sipping his drink while perched quietly on the seat along from me, Frank filtered in a question, more I suspect to break the tension than to start any serious conversation.

"You glad you joined aircrew, Phil?" he asked, with a smile to back up the query.

I pondered that one for a moment, deciding on a throw-away answer to go along with his throw-away question.

"I wasn't doing anything else anyway, Frank," I answered, matching his smile with one of my own.

If I told you the real story, Frankieboy, I thought, you wouldn't believe me. Either that or you would take me for some kind of nut. After all, I had no great love for flying. Joining aircrew was just a casual whim of the moment. They had this war going on at the time, and flying through it seemed a much better idea than walking or crawling through it.

PART ONE

THE AMATEURS

CHAPTER ONE

How About This War Then?

The careless politics of the 1930s, together with someone's insatiable lust for power, were about to meet head-on. This fracas would come to be known as World War Two.

I smiled a little as I marched into the offices of the Ministry of Labour in Dundee to "answer the call".

"Army, Navy, or Air Force?"

The question seemed to explode through the grill-work, the civil servant posing the query barely looking up.

"Pilot," I said with out-of-character firmness, my answer jarring its way across the counter.

"You can't just ask to be a pilot," he came back; thinking, I'm sure, but not saying out loud, "because that sort of reply will ruin my lovely form". "Anyway," he continued, and quoted from fact, "all aircrew personnel have to be volunteers."

"That's true," I replied, "and I did volunteer two months ago. So far I've had no response to my application."

There was a pause, while we both retired to our neutral mental corners.

"All right," he said very slowly, drawing out the words as he measured his reply, "here's what I'll do. I'll tick against 'Air Force', and add an overrider note stating that you have already volunteered for aircrew. How about that?"

One month later I was ordered to report to Edinburgh to undergo the full nausea of an aircrew medical.

I couldn't help thinking that the Royal Air Force had a real problem on its hands. How did they figure on making a front-line, gung-ho pilot out of the sort of material I provided — a shy, reticent, non-belligerent country boy? My instant reaction to finding a spider in the bath is to coax it onto a piece of paper, then carry it outside to set it free. On top of that, and this is a secret I have kept to myself until now, I had no great passion for either flying or flying machines. They just happened to be one of the more attractive alternatives offered on the day. After all, I had no desire to go charging across another Somme.

I approached the Aircrew Selection Board in Hanover Street, Edinburgh, at 0900 hours on 22 January 1942. The tests, assessments and examinations would go on for the full working day.

First up, there was a written examination. Mathematics occupied the first hour, with two topical questions to be answered in essay form filling in hour two. Part three called for twenty general knowledge questions. The rest of the forenoon was ours to use as we would — all fifteen minutes of it.

After lunch, the medics had their turn. The toughest test was that for the lungs, heart, blood pressure and nerve centres, the biggest hurdle here being the mercury test.

To ascertain the soundness and capacity of the lungs was the object of this exercise, and the equipment involved was really disarmingly simple in construction. It consisted of an elongated U-tube, each side of which measured twelve inches. There was a rubber tube and mouthpiece attached to the open end of one leg of the U-tube, with a thin line painted high on the side of the second leg. Lurking in the lower regions of the equipment was a generous dollop of that heaviest of all liquids, mercury. We were asked to blow the mercury up the second leg of the tube until it reached the painted line. It was the final part of the request, the sting in the tail, that cut everyone down to size. With one breath, we were to hold the mercury at the line for sixty seconds. At thirty seconds I was beginning to feel concerned; by forty seconds my heart was really pounding it out; by fifty seconds I could feel the blood flushing my cheeks; by sixty seconds I was about to blow apart.

"That's fine," said the medic.

I barely heard him. Cleverly slotted away in the middle of both of these inspections was the main pivot of the day, the spark plug that would really, really decide if each one of us had a future, indeed a place, in the high-flying, exciting, dangerous world of the Royal Air Force in wartime. This was the Selection Board.

Since I had received the all-important certificate at the end of the day, recommending me for pilot training, if was clear that the one man Selection Board had given me the thumbs-up.

I could only wait and hope.

CHAPTER
TWO

The Course Gets Coarser

Scars of the initiation battle were beginning to show.

"You know, Jock, I don't think the Germans have a thing to worry about. Put all fifty of this shower into a paper bag, and they'd be hard pushed to fight their way back out."

This assessment came from a room-mate, and it was a difficult one to knock down. There we were, shot full of holes to accommodate endless inoculations; poncing around in uniforms that only fitted where they touched; and having a really aching, crippling, blistering time breaking in new boots.

"We shouldn't have joined," was about the best comeback I could think of at the time. One feature that was allowing us to clutch a modest dash of pride was that little white flash in our wedge caps that identified us as potential aircrew.

Someone in the next room, obviously a someone with stars in his eyes, suggested that we should move on from here as quickly as possible to start flying training.

"If we leave it too long," he reasoned, "the war will be over before we can get in there."

My mate and I looked at each other and smiled.

"Bloody hell!" he said in an undertone. "Where do they get them from? Just because we've proved we have no known disease, this comedian thinks it's time for us to be sprung on an unsuspecting public."

"He must have seen *Dawn Patrol* with Errol Flynn and David Niven," suggested another chap in the corner of our room.

The hierarchy was not going to "spring" us anywhere; ease us in gently and discreetly maybe, but certainly not spring us. There was no point in damaging the public's morale any more than necessary.

Instead of sending us straight to an Initial Training Wing (ITW) — the natural progressional step at this time — someone had wedged in a new course, an Elementary Training Wing (ETW). This terminology turned out to be a simple euphemism for a toughening-up camp, a stall tactic, a time-killer. The camp was located in Shropshire and it had nothing to do with flying.

As we marched more than a mile from the railway station at the little Shropshire town of Ludlow to the camp site, the rain bucketed down. Our kit bags were getting heavier and soggier as we trudged along, the water and our morale trickling steadily down into our still-to-be-broken-in, shiny boots. Many times over the next few weeks, the same plaintive plea would echo across the compound: "But what the hell has this got to do with flying?"

Everything was out there in the open. We had our meals in the open; the cooking was done in the open, and the work we were assigned was out in the open. We even washed in the open — both ourselves and our soiled clothing. Toilet seats and the buckets they topped were right there in the open, and we would drill and play sports in the open. From where I was standing, this was just about the most open place I had ever seen.

Ten years from now we would laugh at all of this.

Curiously enough, though, this push-it-to-the-limit camp was creating a powerful presence in our little canvas home, an unshakeable *esprit de corps*. By the end of our three-week stint, the eight boys in our tent were like blood brothers.

One line of normality ran through this bizarre part of our training. In every group there are always those whose stars seem to shine brighter, those who stir up the mud. Without doubt, Jack Evans and Bill Warner were our star performers, especially Jack.

Originating from London, Jack was a pocket-sized ball of fire. Even the camp, with all its frustrations and discomforts, could not neutralise this bouncy personality. Certainly it did nothing to put the chopper on his very active social career. Large as life, Jack would roll into the bland country town that was Ludlow, and there spill his happy-go-lucky natural charms all over the place. His rather short stature was quickly balanced out by his mop of black hair, moustache and Cagney-type image. I could imagine the local girls melting like ice-cream in the face of his licentious come-on. Jack could imagine it too, and he waded through the town talent, knee deep. Honesty was his strength.

While the other Romeos professed true love, Jack professed true lust, and it worked every time.

15

Admittedly, he attracted like-on-like, a reality that did nothing to upset our boy one little bit. Francie, he admitted to us, his blood brothers, was his favourite. This maiden could match our boy's casual approach move for move. He liked that.

"There would be no point pushing out the old line of goo to a girl like Francie," he explained. "One night, for example, when I was pounding her anatomy into the mattress, there she was enjoying every earth-shattering minute of it, while at the same time eating fish and chips! The night before that it was an apple."

Bill Warner was an equally soft touch for the maidens; though quieter and less flamboyant in style, he was good for a smile here and there just the same.

"Man, oh man!" he blurted out one night as he bundled in through the tent flaps. It was right on lights-out time. We could see by his expression that he had run things a bit close. "I've got to be more careful in future."

It was the sort of remark that immediately clicked seven sets of ears into high gear, all flapping back and ready to receive. There were fleeting visions of irate fathers with shotguns and anxious people asking for blood tests. What built up the curiosity was the wild idea of Bill being anything but careful. This was Mr Careful himself.

"Well," came the impatient nudge-along from somewhere around the tentpole, "don't keep us hanging by our eyelashes. What happened?"

Wearing his ever-present, serious expression, Bill fell back onto his bed space and explained.

"I'd been in a tangle for most of the night with that kinky little brunette from the post office . . . By the way, talking about her, anyone else been there?"

"Bill," the impatient, long-suffering jostle was coming from Jack, "we're all fired up on the heart-stopping brush with whatever disaster it was that nearly nobbled you. We can get back between the legs of the post office later. Get on with the story."

"Oh yes," Bill agreed, nodding. "Well, on the way back to the tent here I stopped off at that open tap just inside the camp perimeter. If you must know, I was washing all the vital bits between my legs. What I didn't notice was the Orderly Sergeant coming up behind me. I nearly shit a brick. If you were to ask, I'd say I think I got everything out of sight before he reached me, but man, was it closer than close."

Once again, the mental picture had the place in an uproar.

Mercifully, the deviation that was the Elementary Training Wing would soon become just an entry on my record card. The amorous antics of our tent gang certainly helped me understand why the medics insisted on these apparently endless "Free From Infection" (FFI) checks everywhere our young and red-blooded hopefuls went. In the not-too-distant future, I was to be singled out from the line in one of these famous checks.

17

CHAPTER
THREE

Pilots? Ten-A-Penny!

By the end of 1942, Britain and her allies were pushing out fully trained pilots like sausages from a meat factory; so efficiently, in fact, that their proliferation had become a positive embarrassment. Pilots were ten-a-penny.

One category in short supply was that of navigator, the brains of the bomber fleet. He was the crew member expected to continue plotting courses and measuring tracks while all hell was breaking loose right outside his window.

My stay at an ITW was to have more surprises than a snap election. There was more bullshit flying around this place than there were promises in an election. We were at Babbacombe atop the two hundred-foot cliffs of Devon's lovely south coast. Ian Lockhart and I, two of the "blood brothers" from our tent at Ludlow, were posted here. The other six "brothers" were sent to an establishment on the Welsh coast which specialised in training air gunners. Five of the six disappeared into the system, but I hadn't heard the last of Jack Evans.

ITW, though, was no jacked-up, let's-while-away-a-little-time setup like Ludlow. This was one of the big steps along the way. Either the triers got this one right or they could kiss their wings goodbye.

The more we listened to the Commanding Officer's opening address, the more we recognised ourselves for what we were: bunnies. I was not only one of the bunnies, I was a bunny who didn't like to kill things! By the end of the three-month course at this place I would be given two sharp lessons. What surprised me was the source of the tuition. It would be courtesy of the Germans. Lesson number one was to come along in a few days' time.

There we were on a lovely autumn day, twenty very new and raw aircrew cadets, sitting and standing around the sun-drenched park in this very beautiful Devon resort. The high cliffs overlooking the dramatic sweep of the bay were just across the road from the park gate. Each one of us, pencil and notebook in hand, was taking a turn to decipher and/or record the letters being blinked out at us from an Aldis lamp located in an office building about a quarter of a mile away. We were super keen, quite convinced that we were the air aces of tomorrow. With such concentration and dedication, the new sound thundering toward us had to work just that little bit harder to get through. Then we heard it.

The unmistakable stuttering, pumping sound of cannon shelling erupted from up and over the high cliff tops — and it was coming straight for us! Farce — ever the opportunist — decided to mingle with the tragedy. The nearest tree to our group, if challenged, just might have provided cover for one, but it certainly had no

19

hope of sheltering all the frightened, potential heroes who stampeded in behind it. The sight must have been a classic.

Two Focke-Wulf 190s flew overhead at about fifty feet, cannons chattering, anti-personnel bombs hanging menacingly from either wing. A few seconds later we heard these bombs exploding. The Aldis lamp lesson was immediately abandoned. All of us were marched back to our hotels on the sea front.

One of the bombs had hit St John's Church, while several of the others had scored bull's-eyes on the Royal Air Force Hospital a little farther inland. All aircrew cadets were ordered to help. Some were sent directly to the scene of the disaster, others to prepare our beds for possible use. Mercifully, I was to be a bedmaker.

Some of the stories returning with my colleagues from the devastation were traumatic, providing instant meaning to the anything-goes concept of total war.

On the beautifully cut and tended lawn of the hospital grounds lay a corpse with neither legs nor arms. Inside the building a lady, possibly a member of the Women's Auxiliary Air Force, had been in the bath. Now she had no stomach and no head. And so the stories continued.

Intelligence suggested that these flights by the Luftwaffe pilots were a "passing out test" at the end of their flight training. There would be the wave-top "Geronimo" over the Channel at full blast, a quick zoom up and over the cliffs at a relatively safe part of the English coastline, then all bullets, shells and bombs unleashed as productively and quickly as possible before screaming back to France as fast as their wings could carry them. Our radar operators would hardly notice the blips on their screens.

CHAPTER
FOUR

Bowels To You, Too!

"Crap into a bottle!?"

"Be serious, Philip me boy. Surely no one's going to suggest to us that we start our flying careers by shitting into a bottle!"

"To start with, have you given fair attention to the size of these things? Even the Americans with their Norden bombsight would have difficulty hitting a target that size."

So the banter to'd and fro'd across the barrack room; laughter, guffaws, and broad grins spiced things along. I could see that the boys were really enjoying themselves, the orators wallowing in their doubt and disbelief. And why not? There hadn't been much to laugh about over the past few days.

I continued to take the tiny bottles from my uniform pocket and line them up on the table, one-by-one. They were small enough to be sample phials for very expensive perfume. When the oral crossfire had dampened down, I'd have another go at trying to break through the wall of incredulity.

Problems had started to simmer about three days before: grumbling stomach twinges at first, then the isolated case of diarrhoea, the whole comedy finally degenerating into "screamers' paradise". Aircrew cadets were buckling up with stomach-ache like saplings in a storm, and diarrhoea was the only game in town. The flying programme was beginning to feel lots of pain, and that made Head Office sit up and take notice. Flying must go on.

Reaction from the hierarchy was swift and positive, something that always happens when they themselves are beginning to feel the heat. The medics questioned us individually as we reported with the "screams", hoping to find some common link. Finding nothing, they ordered all of us to meet in one of the lecture rooms.

"My bowels aren't just loose, Sir, they're positively promiscuous." This from Jackson who, though physically uncomfortable, could be relied upon for his colourful turn of phrase.

"What do you mean?"

"Well, Sir, when the stomach-ache hits at ground level, the sanctuary of the toilet block has to be sought out very fast. Three thousand feet up in a Tiger Moth, and fifteen minutes from the airfield, could be fatal. Hanging fire for even a few seconds can become a high risk situation."

The Chief Medical Officer smiled and dismissed the group. "I'll get back to you shortly," he assured us.

When I reported to Sick Bay, there had already been a decision. I was right on the spot to act as messenger, to make the judgement known to the boys.

"Take these bottles back to the barracks, Gray, and give one to each cadet who has diarrhoea."

Back at the barracks, the boys listened.

"Are you telling me that our leaders want us to jack off to the bog, do the necessary, and then shove it into one of these microscopic containers?"

"Jacko," I reasoned, "if you — if all of us — want to get this Grading School tiger off our backs, we've got to stop flying off to the nearest 'can' every half hour, and start flying through the clouds again."

"So?"

"So just put a tiny bit of craperoo into the bottle, write your name and last three on the label, and return it to the Sick Bay."

Someone else threw in his pennyworth.

"What will they do then; serve it up with custard?"

"Nope. All samples are to be analysed."

Mercifully, the source of the trouble was picked up fairly quickly by those analysts microscoping their way through our body wastes.

The culprit was the tea.

To save time, and no doubt labour, the cooks didn't bother to make fresh tea for each meal. They just set the urn going in the morning, and then kept piling in more tea and water as the level of the liquid dropped, allowing the huge urn to go on and off the boil throughout the day. The result was a none-too-pleasant tasting concoction which, as a purgative, could leave castor oil for dead. Now that the cause was singled out, the tea improved, flying resumed, and we soon moved away from the diarrhoea syndrome.

This had been a particularly bad time for a plague of the "screamers". Coventry was a watershed in our potential flying careers, a harvesting point for would-be pilots. We were on trial at Southam, a fact which in itself could make most bowel contents turn to water, without any help from "Southam stomach", as this malaise had come to be known.

Up in the air I shone like a beacon. Stalling and steep turns were no problem. I re-started a dead engine in flight several times, boring straight down from 9,000 feet, both sets of magneto switches set to "On", until the motor fired back to life. Spinning — one exercise that stopped a few in their tracks — didn't faze me at all. After the shock of the first spin, I quite enjoyed them. All of us were well aware of the golden rule, namely: "He who throws up in the cockpit, cleans it out afterwards." That seemed fair. Where I kept coming unstuck was in trying to land.

Crunch day arrived and, true to form, it was gusty, squally and wet. Happily, I flew the plane beautifully, getting it back to the airfield through all the clag. This seemed to impress the boss. The landing was no epic, but acceptable.

The contest between the weather and me could be marked as a draw. On this important day, I'd given it my best shot with the head man. Visibility was so bad that Squadron Leader Waller scrubbed the solo run, but made it clear that he marked my card as if I had actually flown solo. How often I wished, in the years to come, that I had gone back at a later date to shake this man's hand.

With this course completed, all we had to do now, while waiting for the gradings to come through, was to find a corner somewhere and die a little each waiting day.

CHAPTER
FIVE

East To West

If I thought I had reached the pits at Coventry, I was due for a rude awakening in Manchester!

Heaton Park.

Now there is a name wartime aircrew knew very well, its pathways and green acres looming large on their highway to the stars. It was within this Manchester playground that aircrew would be grouped into large overseas drafts, to be shipped off to Canada, Rhodesia, or the United States. Most looked upon Heaton Park as a necessary pain in the butt. For me, it was to be a nightmare.

It all started when I committed that greatest of all crimes — I got caught.

While in Dundee on leave, I had been "booked" by a service policeman for wearing my battledress top. Regulation dress off station was "best blue", the regular Air Force uniform. It was a trivial misdemeanour for which I was to pay dearly.

On the fourth day the system nailed me for that dress default, and my world started to crumble. This was an outside charge, as opposed to a local charge, so I had to face a really big wheel — the Station Commander. The punishment was fourteen days' extra duties.

Then, after I had completed seven of the fourteen days, the little organisers in the shadows decided to form a Discip. (Disciplinary) Flight. To bolster its numbers, the authorities decided to add those lucky lads already on jankers. Now, not only did I have seven days' jankers still to go, but I was committed to another fourteen days in the Discip. Flight! This was a tough outfit. While other flights paraded in normal gear, we had to line up with full packs and wearing gas masks. Every time we moved in the park it was at the double while still puffing and sweating inside those gas masks.

My feet were now in a sorry state but the marching and pounding went on.

Once or twice I did feel this shivery, tingling sensation around my middle, but I put it down to the non-stop, hot/cold treatment. Back at the billet, I noticed this curious, small, bubble-like thing that had suddenly appeared on the left side of my waist. I covered the bubble with a piece of elastoplast and forgot it.

The pace was beginning to tell. Even the walk back to the billet was agony.

Suddenly, a Canadian draft! The kick-off was to be an en masse Free From Infection (FFI) examination of 2,000 cadets to pick out those who had contracted a dose of venereal disease while spreading their favours around Manchester.

From time to time the medics would hit the jackpot, and one of the cadets would be directed to join the select little band of suspects in the corner of the hall. There would be one mighty cheer from the other cadets in the hall, the incident building up the notoriety of those picked out of the line. Sure enough, when I lined up for the full frontal, that piece of elastoplast stuck out like an Everton supporter at the Liverpool end. Plaster was stripped off, bubble exposed, and without hesitation one of the medics directed me to join the select little group. This time the raucous cheers and knowing grins beamed toward me. I couldn't go to them individually and explain that all I had was a dose of shingles.

Within the hour, I was in Ward 4 of the Squadron Sick Quarters, and for me the Canadian draft was history. Within a further day, bubbles were spreading around my waist like the plague.

Ah yes, I would remember Heaton Park — very well.

On Tuesday, 2 March 1943, we had been given our gradings.

At long weary last, after many hundreds of us had been poured into the gloom of the Heaton Park cinema, all the many pieces from the past were to fall into place.

As the names and gradings came at us, destinies were being dispensed with clinical efficiency in a mere moment in time: "Goodman, 324 — Navigator; Gray, 847 — Pilot; Hanson . . ." One word boomed back at me like a thunderstorm: Pilot.

Five weeks after the last exodus, Heaton Park was gearing up for another big push. It was to be an American draft, news guaranteed to have smiles erupting all around. While Canadian stations had the reputation for being cold, both in temperature and in discipline, American flying schools were supposed to be the end of the rainbow.

For most of us on this move to the west, but oh so specifically for me, one line in the CO's address hit the mark right on the nose. Said he of our stay at Heaton Park: "Never have so many been buggered around so much by so few." I could second that statement, Buster, I thought at the time.

Our conveyance overseas was to be none other than the legendary queen of the Atlantic herself, RMS *Queen Mary*. Not only were we off to the battle-free skies of the United States, but we were going there in style.

"When do we join the convoy?"

John Mitchell directed the question to the crew member who had just come into the cabin. John, like the rest of us, had seen the sixty or so other ships spread all around the huge bay at Gourock.

"This ship, my friend, is the convoy. The *Queen Mary* travels alone at 32 knots, changes her basic course every few minutes, changes the course pattern every half hour. If any U-boat wants to try its luck with that lot, then it's welcome to have a go. Anyway, we are not exactly what you could call defenceless. You should see the hardware we have on the top deck. There are 52 guns up there, everything from pom-poms and 20mm ack-ack through to 3.7 inch and 6 inch naval guns. It's a formidable display."

During the next few days an interesting range of fellow passengers joined the ship. One day behind us were hundreds of prisoners of war, both German and Italian, and although we never saw the Germans again, the Italians were both visible and vocal throughout the voyage. The Italian POWs were always served first in the dining room. This meant that we passed on the stairways, separated only by their armed guards, and the crossfire of insults between the two groups was quite funny.

It was difficult to ignore the Italians and their throw-away, what-the-hell attitude to their situation. They seemed to look upon this war as some kind of joke. Maybe if we had all listened to our Latin cousins, we could have ended up laughing at one another rather than killing one another.

Over the next few days more and more important people joined the cruise. The list included Sir William Beveridge, the architect of social services in Britain; Ernest Bevin, a participant in the formation of the North Atlantic Treaty Organisation; King Haakon of Norway; Winston Churchill; Field Marshal Wavell; Sir Charles Portal — a brilliant airman of World War One, then Chief of Air Staff; Lord Louis Mountbatten; Anthony Eden; Lord Beaverbrook, minister of aircraft production; and, big surprise, Squadron Leader Waller, boss of the Grading School complex at Southam, and possibly the man most responsible for my being aboard.

Throughout the entire voyage we were never without a sizeable protective escort, a mixture of six cruisers and destroyers riding shotgun at all times.

31

On the eleventh day we found United States Coast Guard and police power boats cosseting the ship. The *Queen Mary* had completed her "round the houses" voyage across the Atlantic, side-stepped the U-boats one more time, and was edged into Pier 87, right alongside the berth occupied by the giant liner, the *Normandy*. The French oceanic queen was lying on her side, having burned out the year before and toppled over from the weight of water pumped in to douse the flames.

Our batch of aircrew hopefuls got out of bed aboard the *Queen Mary* and back into bed at Camp Miles Standish in the United States. Coming from war-torn, blacked out, severely rationed, and backs-to-the-wall Britain, we seemed somehow to have squeezed through to the other side of the mirror.

As we danced away the first night, the girls in our arms were gift wrapped in beautiful dresses, the bread holding the sandwiches together was actually white, there were chocolate bars and ice cream in plentiful supply, and everywhere we looked outside there were cars, cars, cars.

None of us actually said it out loud at the time, but the eyes carried the message: Please! — don't even try to pinch me. I don't want to wake up! Given time, we could learn to live with a war like this.

CHAPTER
SIX

Get On Your Mark

From there we moved up to Moncton, Canada. After two weeks spent reorganising, we headed south-west to Arizona by rail, now attired from neck to toe in US issue uniform. The one piece of Royal Air Force clothing retained was the wedge cap with its coveted white flash. Our goal was Falcon Field, just outside Mesa, Arizona, home of No 4 British Flying Training School.

Mesa is in the south-west quadrant of Arizona, Falcon Field lying flush along the carpet valley of the Sonoran desert. At the outset there would be one hundred of us in Course 16; eighty-three cadets from the Royal Air Force and seventeen US Army Air Corps cadets.

The tools of our trade were the Stearman and Harvard aircraft, both lined up there on the tarmac, both still in their original silver colour. They looked very flyable and inviting.

We rode to the field in an open-sided, no-windows bus. Our living accommodation included an outdoor swimming pool, floodlit above and below the waterline; a comfortable lounge; pool room with jukebox and

Pepsi machines; and soft drinks and ice cream servery in the old drugstore style — all alien stuff perhaps, but oh so civilised.

Come Monday morning, 31 May 1943, and the serious business of flying finally got under way. Mr Lockridge was the instructor assigned to our group of four.

Here we had another surprise. All of these American instructors were civilians, despite their official Army Air Corps uniforms. There was no rank insignia on their shoulder epaulettes. We learned very clearly and very fast that there was nothing "civilian" or half-baked about their tuition. They were highly qualified professionals.

Our Mr Lockridge was typical. He wanted positive, no-nonsense flying. Mistakes he would accept, but he would not expect to see that same mistake again. I could work with a guy like this, even accepting his taciturn, dour manner. Many of the most important gems Mr Lockridge offered were his asides, the pieces of advice that were not in the instruction manual. These were, in fact, bits of advice that did not always meet with the approval of his fellow instructors. He warned me about this possibility. He warned me, and I listened. Down through the weeks, months, and years to follow, these asides would become golden rules for me. They must have saved my tail many times.

Whatever the situation, he would suggest, keep shortening the odds in your own favour. Fly as tight and as close a circuit as you can. That way, if your engine cut, you could still fly the machine back onto the runway. No problem. If this practice places you too high on the final approach, just side-slip or "fishtail" (that's a double side-slip) the height away. In the years to follow, I became so adept at this side-slipping caper that, forty years later, one examiner asked me specifically to carry out a longer, conventional approach. I smiled. Mr Lockridge would have smiled, too.

Another of those famous asides was the "looking around" gambit.

"Keep rubber necking all the time," he advised, "and be aware of everything that is going on around you. If it's a case of rubber necking or keeping all the instruments right on the button, to hell with the instruments. That thing you are sitting on, it's called your ass; it will tell you most of the time what the instruments are saying. Continual looking around during normal flying could save you from an embarrassing situation. During combat, it could save you from getting a bullet in the back of your head. Think about it!"

Many months later, when people were trying very, very hard to kill us, I did think about this advice. Nearly forty-five years later, and still flying, I go on thinking about it. I remember Mr Lockridge. He was the first to churn out that old favourite for me: There are lots of old pilots, there are lots of bold pilots; but there are very few old, bold pilots.

The Stearmans, with their great wing surface and light weight, were susceptible to heat-wave trickery. I fell for it once and ground looped when one of my wings hit the deck. Planes taxied into each other right there on the ground, their pilots blinded by sudden whip-ups of sand.

The real fun, of course, was way up there in the air, right away from the dust. Mr Lockridge loved aerobatics so his pupils got free rein on this type of flying.

One bit of advice: when first starting aerobatics and elongated spinning, it's best to lay off the greasy pies, ice-cream and Coke just before take-off. Otherwise they could all come up a whole lot faster than they went down.

There is something about the spin that carries a fatal fascination, possibly because of the air of uncertainty that rides along with it.

"First we'll go up to five or six thousand feet, have a good look below to see if the airspace is clear, making sure that we are well strapped in. Remember, we are in an open cockpit. Any plane will lose interest if its engine cuts, so, make it do just that; pull the throttle right back. At the same time, pull the nose of the aircraft up at a fairly steep angle, and wait while the speed falls away. Just when the plane is about to drop its nose and go into what it thinks will be a straight dive, kick on one of the rudders and send the nose over to one side. There you have it; you've set up a spin."

There is a danger that you might let the whole thing mesmerise you.

Approximately fifty per cent of our time at Falcon Field would be spent in classrooms. There would be examinations and tests throughout the course, ending with the final Wings Examination. Failure here, regardless of any prowess in the air, would mean a "wash-out" from the course.

But then, let's be practical, no one comes all the way to the US of A just to flog in flying hours. There were many beautiful people to see. There were many beautiful places to visit.

We could see Superstition Mountain from the airfield, a place where the spirits of Indians long gone now guarded the legendary buried gold of the Apaches. Scattered around the State are the Petrified Forest, Canyon Lake, Roosevelt Dam, the infamous Painted Desert, Monument Valley, ancient Indian cliff dwellings, and the famous Grand Canyon. They were all fabulous sights familiar to the cadets of Course 16, though we had monitored their beauty and interest only as we flew overhead. Common sense told us that we owed ourselves a closer look at such wonders. Destiny might never bring us this way again.

All of us were around the magical notch of twenty-one, most raring to be "where it was at". Matched against those places of natural beauty and human ingenuity, California's Pacific Coast knew very well it had the really big one on offer: Hollywood. For fools like us, it was the only place to go.

Invitations were non-stop. Would we like to see the Douglas Aircraft factory? Would we like to see Paramount Picture Studios? At the latter we saw the cut-down-to-size house the studio had built for Shirley Temple when she was a child star. We saw, too, the "Props" Library, consisting of single front facades or profiles, i.e. just the front facing walls of buildings. These are still used to simulate such settings as western towns or historical scenes. It was all good make-believe stuff. How could the Grand Canyon stand up to competition like this? Now each leave from Falcon Field we'd be back to LA just as fast as our thumbs could earn us a ride.

We were sure we would go and see the Petrified Forest one day . . . someday . . . maybe!

CHAPTER
SEVEN

The Game Shows Its Muscle

It was difficult to take life seriously after the socialising overkill of Hollywood. In life we were about to discover that the reality of sudden and violent death is not restricted to players in the front line. Cadets, too, can be taken out in many different ways.

Mr Piercy was our instructor for intermediate and advanced training.

On the night of Friday, 13 August, Course 15's Gorman took his Harvard to about 200 feet when the engine cut. He was caught in the split-second decision of will-I or won't-I turn back. At that height there was, categorically, no choice. Every book in the trade quite rightly directs the pilot to land straight ahead. Unfortunately, he tried to turn back to the sanctuary of the airfield, stalled, spun in, and was killed.

A few days later the carnage continued. Two planes collided in the circuit: a cadet in his first solo in one, the other an instructor/pupil duo. Both were in Stearmans. The instructor and his pupil were killed. The vexation was about to move up a few notches.

Carroll was the pilot, an American cadet from the South, his conversation always clipped and laconic. In the heat of the day he could invariably be found lying on top of his bed, naked, with only his hat on to shield his eyes from the sun. Most of us liked Carroll and his disdain for bullshit. Apparently his engine had cut out when he was quite a distance from the airfield, the one redeeming factor being that he had a fair amount of height. At this point we all heard the "Mayday! Mayday! Mayday!" emergency call on the radio, given in the typical, unhurried Carroll fashion.

In any emergency, the Control Tower will always pour out a continuous stream of assurances to calm the pilot of a stricken aircraft. They do the best they can, which is to keep on talking. The advisers are still down there on the ground in their warm, safe control tower; the pilot is still up there in his ailing aircraft, hanging on by his eyelashes. No one would ever say this out loud, of course.

Correction, no one but Carroll would dare say it; that changed this emergency into a classic. Every pilot listening in, instructor and cadet alike, must have doubled up with laughter.

As the stricken AT6A did its slow, agonising, engineless glide toward the distant haven of Falcon Field, the goo from the Tower continued unabated: "You'll be all right. You still have plenty of height. Hang in there."

Then came the clincher. What the controller said was: "You're all right, Number Three Four. We have you visual. We can see you now."

The Southern drawl from the cockpit cut straight back, and pulled that one right down to size . . .

"I can see you too," iced back Carroll, "but that doesn't do me any f------ good."

Oh yes, friend Carroll did make the base — just — by landing downwind on the runway in use. Yes, he did get a wrap over the knuckles for using a heavy, four-letter expletive on the air. But, you'll have to believe it, Tuesday the seventeenth wasn't finished with us yet. Manderson came waltzing in to land with his undercarriage still retracked, and ended up screaming along the runway, wheels up, sparks scything out in all directions. He bent the plane quite a bit.

The day may have ended, but the incidents had not. Five days later the Course 15 boys set off on their four-day, 2,000-mile, final cross-country exercise to Texas. A few of them misread their compasses and ended up 150 miles inside Mexico. The Mexicans held on to the strays for a day or two, and then packed them back to Arizona.

As the circus continued, Course 17 set a new record by ground looping four of their Stearmans in one day. Loveless, one of "our" Americans on Course 16, had his Harvard engine cut while he was way out over the desert and, carrying out the correct procedure, landed, wheels retracted, in the sand and scrub. He got away with it.

For the record, those pilots I mentioned earlier who ended up in Mexico had their recommendations for commissions withdrawn.

Course 16, though, was coming near the end of its stint at Falcon Field. Time now for the heavy stuff: the five-ship formation flying; the long, long cross-country flights; and some concentrated night flying.

There were lessons to be learned here, some of them salutary indeed.

I don't know where our chiefs got them from, but these American flying instructors were good; they were very, very good indeed. Being so good, they expected their pupils to be just that much better than would possibly prove to be the case. The business of formation flying was a fair example.

There would be five aircraft involved in each group. Our own instructor, Mr Piercy, put it on the line for our group.

"Let's get this clear right from the start. When we say 'formation flying', we mean just that: five planes getting in there really close and flying as if they are one plane. Five aircraft flying in the same general direction is not formation flying. Get your wingtip right in behind the wing of the plane on which you are formatting, so close that you can scrape the paint off the side of his fuselage with your wingtip. I want total, razor edge concentration. And here's the incentive. We will keep at it until we all get it right, whether it takes one go or five hundred goe's. It's up to you. But if you want them to pin those wings on your chest . . ." The rest was left unsaid.

We concentrated, we worked, we sweated, and we finally got that five-ship formation flying just dandy, right on the button, and it felt great to be part of such a group.

As before, though, the diversions and grief continued unabated.

Came the fateful night of 29 October 1943. It was a Friday, and Course 16 had the night sky to itself over Falcon Field. But if I thought that was the main event of the evening, I was due for one big punch in the face. There was an air of tragedy stamped across every face in the room. Nobby Clark and Chamberlain, riding together in their cross-country exercise, were way overdue. Meantime, the Highway Patrol had called in to report that they had seen a plane crash near Maricopa. We were to find out later that the Harvard had apparently clipped the tail unit of a Liberator bomber and then continued on, spinning into the ground. There was no great damage to the bigger plane.

So Course 16 had come face-to-face with real tragedy at last.

Hours later, still subdued and fighting to cope with the realisation that the chopper had hit Course 16, we got another boomer. As we were settling down to fitful sleep, a clerk from the Control Tower shook us back to life. Had any of us seen Ginger Lewis? He had reported back to the Tower when over the field at the completion of his cross-country, and then had virtually disappeared. Oh no! Dear Lord, not Ginger! He was also one of the six in our room, his bed area right opposite my space. Of all the cadets on the course, this amiable Londoner must have been one of the most popular. I could never ever remember seeing Ginger without a big broad smile fronting his open easy manner.

Next morning there was good news and bad. Ginger had been spotted by an early morning search plane, the wreckage of his Harvard spread over a fair area of one of the auxiliary landing grounds used by Williams Field, an American flying training school close by. Although badly injured, he had managed to spring his parachute and wrap it around himself as protection against the cold night air. We could only hope and let Ginger fight this one out by himself. As we were told next day, it was a fight he had lost. Arthur (Ginger) Lewis died on Saturday, 30 October 1943, almost exactly twenty-four hours after his plane had hit the deck. He had simply forgotten to readjust his altimeter to local barometric pressure.

I was a pallbearer twice in three days, Saturday for Nobby Clark, and Monday for Ginger. Even now, after so many years, their faces appear very easily out of my recall. I can still see Nobby's concerned look as we conversed in the CO's room at Babbacombe when he asked me how I thought I would front up to the killing game. I will always see Ginger's ready smile and hear his happy quips at life.

Most of us were just making up flying hours. On one ride back to Falcon Field, I did fourteen slow rolls in a straight line, aware that my days over the free and easy scenes of this beautiful American state were all but over for the moment.

The big day was Friday, 3 December 1943. At a huge Wings Passing Out Parade at the US Army's Williams Field, various flights of Chinese, American and British cadets received their wings. The Americans who had trained at Falcon Field received both the American and the Royal Air Force Wings.

For many reasons, the number of our group leaving No 4 British Flying Training School had been trimmed. Many had been eliminated as unfit to carry on with the course; and many had been eliminated because of breaches of the rules; some had been filtered back to a later course; three were to stay behind for ever in the little cemetery not far from the airfield.

We steamed out of Mesa railway station at 6p.m. on 6 December 1943.

CHAPTER
EIGHT

The Road Back

The first leg home started off in the heat of Arizona, USA, and ended up knee-deep in the snow and ice of Moncton, New Brunswick, Canada. Within five days we were moving down the Hudson River aboard RMS *Mauritania*.

We had just taken a few disembarkation paces off the ship when reality crowded our lives. The port was Gourock Bay on Scotland's west coast. There was a steady drizzle to match the cold breeze cutting across at us from the north-east. The train we boarded was soon drumbeating south, its carriages overheated, the lights dimmed to black-out standards, the smell of rain-soaked great coats hanging heavily in the air. Baked beans on toast, blacked-out comfortless streets, wailing sirens, two ounces of butter per ration book, the peculiar throbbing engines of enemy aircraft, uniformed service personnel of many countries, Vera Lynn and those blue birds over the white cliffs of Dover, rubble-strewn bomb sites, overcrowded passenger trains — this was the reality of Britain in 1943.

The British had learned to live with the fact that the front line was everywhere.

Personally, I was having a really hard time trying to walk back into this world of harsh realism that was Britain at war. The open skies we had experienced in our American flying had ill-prepared us for the crowded, danger-laden, meteorological nightmare of the skies over Great Britain.

There we were, cold and wet and not being fêted by anyone. The important thing, though, was that this was our island, and we would do our very best to make sure that no one put an alien trademark on it.

Mid-February and I was back once more to Harrogate Spa, our accommodation venue this time being the huge Majestic Hotel complex right in the centre of town. Recognising faces from the past brought two sergeant pilots from Falcon Field, Ian Maclellan and Bob Henderson, into focus.

Harrogate was obviously some kind of high-powered clearing station, because there were pilots zeroing in here from all over; Canada, Rhodesia and the United States, to name but three.

We now found ourselves fronting up before another one of those most critical of all parleys for wartime aircrew — a Selection Board. Each of these affairs happened but twice to most of us, once to get into aircrew — in my case Edinburgh — and once to decide into which arm of aircrew we would be directed. When it was my turn to make that lonely trip into the room to face the Selection Board, I asked for fighters. I was told very politely that my chances of driving single-engine day machines was nothing to minus zero.

The big show was on one more time. I dropped my slacks and underpants around my ankles and lifted my shirt front way up to give the quack the benefit of the full frontal exposure.

"The whole thing is bloody crude, isn't it?" complained Ian Anderson, as we headed back to the hotel.

"The FFI striptease shouldn't worry you by now, Ian," I consoled. "You must surely have been through that little burlesque show plenty of times by now."

"What the hell, specifically, are they looking for anyway?" Ian continued, completely ignoring my input to the conversation. "To see if something has dropped off?"

"No, I hardly think that is the object of the exercise," I laughed, "but rather to see if something has grown on, like say blisters, sores, or bumps. Show them something they didn't expect to see, and that would really make their day."

Still grumbling and murmuring away to himself, Ian took his fit of pique out on a couple of innocent stones lying there on the pavement, kicking and skeetering them off helter-skelter into the roadway.

Now that the Selection Board had been dealt with, the good old-fashioned ho-hum business of the system was having the time of its bullshitting life.

The Royal Air Force Regiment would reduce us to ribbons on their toughening-up course at Whitley Bay, its secrets hidden in the sand dunes and tall flax-type grass along the town's sea front. For an encore, they would swing in with their punishing route marches of five, ten, and up to twenty-one miles at a whack. The Administration Section would then lead us through the tangle of all there was to know about discipline, the duties of an orderly sergeant, the parts of administration we should know, and some interesting facts about the Officers' Training Units (OTU). To be fair to our leaders, the OTU prospect may well have been the object of this whole exercise. We had no way of knowing.

Finally, the ground staff sergeants would have their say with arms training, precision drill at the ITW criterion of 140 paces to the minute, and lots and lots of physical training. By the end of the four weeks there was every possibility that we would be so fit, we'd be fit for sod all. We could see we were in for a merry time.

"I picked up a new pair of boots just before arriving here and they're giving me hell." The complainer was Don Elsdon, and we all knew just how he felt. This was no place to break in a new pair of boots.

From the next front room on the ground floor of our Links Avenue detached house, we could hear a spirited practised run of one of the great pieces of poetry of World War Two. It was entitled *Eskimo Nell*, and Alex Fisher was the one belting it out.

By the end of the four weeks, each one of us could strip down a Browning machine gun and speedily put it together again, naming each part as we handled it. On the firing ranges at practice time, the safest place to be was right behind the target. I doubt that any of us could have hit a hangar door at ten feet.

Examination time ended it all, and my results ran true to form. Indoors, I got 83 per cent for the General Duties paper and 89 per cent for Administration. Outdoors, I got nine out of twenty for the drill test. The solution was obvious: if our leaders wanted value for money from me, they would have to get me into one of their aeroplanes as quickly as possible in the skies over Britain.

CHAPTER
NINE

The Home Run

The stark difference between our previous playground over Arizona and this aerial battleground over the United Kingdom was a wee bit frightening. Once in the air over Falcon Field in the American state, especially at night, we could see the lights of the next town or city fifty to a hundred miles away. There were very few lights twinkling back at us now from the blacked-out land below us.

Survival conscious as ever, we got all the really important priorities dropped into line quickly. What we had to discover straight away, from those on the more senior courses, were such important things as: where are the best places in town to find food?; which are the most favoured establishments for drinks?; and — the big one — where would we find the girls? Obviously we were keen exponents of the one-track mind syndrome.

On completion of the very first hour of circuits and general rehabilitation flying in the De Havilland 82a, the Tiger Moth, the instructor, Warrant Officer Brownley, and I were trundling back across the wet tarmac to the flight room. Both of us had parachutes slung across our shoulders and were struggling for conversation. In answer to his fill-in question about my future, I told him about the vague promise of single-engine instruction I had been given at Harrogate during the Selection Board interview.

"Well," he reasoned, "far be it from me to pound your hopes into the mud. Think about this very course you are now churning through. It is called pre-AFU instruction, suggesting that AFU itself is the next idea in mind. And that, my friend, means light twin-engine aircraft. Light twins are a lead on to heavy twins, which in turn could be a lead on to the big boys — the heavy four-engine bombers. With a bit of luck, you could even find yourself lording it around in the Avro Lancaster, the end of the pilot's rainbow."

What the more experienced pilot was trying to tell me was that I was already on the home run. It would seem that the home run would slot me right into Bomber Command.

Next morning, maybe as a sort of consolation prize for the home truths he had dropped on my head the night before, WO Brownley skipped the three-hour requirement of dual instruction and let me loose solo after only a further 35 minutes' dual flying. Soon, and more as solo flying than dual, the pair of us dropped into a comfortable routine of aerobatics and local map reading all over the place.

Easter had presented itself right on cue, trailing three days of leave in its wake. The proviso attached to the leave was that we must not travel farther than twenty miles from base, and that we must leave a positive destination address. No one explained why the conditions were so specific, because our three-week course still had a long way to go to completion.

Rather than appear a stay-at-home deadbeat, I picked a place called Aspatria from the map at random, and gave my destination as the YMCA there. I did, of course, stay at "home" (the base). This was a big mistake.

During the Easter break a posting had come through for me on the Friday, and Administration had tried to contact me. One, they could not find me in Aspatria, and two, they discovered there was no YMCA in that place. Despite the ironic fact that I was right there on the station all the time, a charge was laid against me. So, cap in hand, I had to do the quick march caper before the CO, and got a reprimand placed on my record card for the trouble I had caused.

Ah well, there were many good things trailing along in the wake of the telling-off. Warrant Officer Brownley and I had a whole lot more time to churn up the skies with aerobatics when the cloud would allow it, followed by several long cross-country flights, whether or not the cloud would allow it.

Light tanks, heavy tanks, ammunition trucks, mobile landing craft, field guns, anti-aircraft guns, anonymous crates stacked high under green tarpaulins — all of these things had been convoying south past our front door at Carlisle throughout our last week's stay at Kingston Airport. They must have been parked all over Scotland, because the procession went on relentlessly, endlessly, day and night. Somebody, somewhere, was spoiling for a fight, and they were making very sure that their side would not be caught short on the day.

The fabled Second Front was obviously coming closer. Every tank and landing craft that rolled by was underlining the rules for today's war in the air. In 1940, single-engine aircraft were for people with their backs to the wall. By 1944, bombers and the big stick were the tools of those seeking retribution and moving on to the offensive. As we rolled through the gates of Calveley Airfield in Cheshire, we liked the look of the twin-engine Oxford aircraft, machines having the magical number of engines that could be part of our passport into the cockpit of the fashionable chariot of this ever-changing war — the heavy bomber.

As I was about to find out, the Service had no monopoly on surprises. Telephoning home in the evening, I learned that one of my school friends, Bob Cunningham, had been killed in action while flying over the Third Reich. An air bomber with Bomber Command, he had "bought it" on only his third operational trip over Germany. At times the pressure began to show through the cracks.

Weary after three stints in the air, I bent down inside the "office" of the Oxford's cabin, my fingers seeking out the engine cut-out lever at my feet. Unfortunately, I had forgotten to pull on the brake before ducking out of sight. By the time I looked up again, the aircraft was moving steadily down the incline of the parking area, straight toward another Oxford passing by on the perimeter track. I rammed on the brakes, the other aircraft dusting its wingtips past my nose. Two more seconds and my propellers would have been chewing into the other machine, smearing the consequences all over my record card. The ground staff sighed visibly with relief as my crate shuddered to a halt. So did I.

Next morning I pulled off the kind of boomer that makes pilots everywhere want to crawl into a corner and put the lights out. Still chasing too many flying hours, I taxied to the wrong end of the runway, and was solemnly set to take off downwind. A red Aldis flashing urgently from the Tower brought me back to reality. All exciting stuff, but none of this was earning us any Brownie points.

PART TWO

THE APOSTLES

CHAPTER
ONE

The New Order Of Things

Suddenly we were on a roll. It was bonus time.

"As far as I can see," Jackson smiled, "no one seems to be greatly interested any more in what sort of flying we do up there, just as long as we bring the Oxfords back in one piece."

"After all," Murray reasoned, "we've all completed the conversion. All that's left for us now is to pile on the official number of hours."

The same footloose benevolence followed us to base and into our free time. We could come and go more or less as we pleased. Maybe someone up there was testing our self-discipline.

We were like little boys let out of school early. Most of us still had five to six hours solo to fly to reach the required hours. How we filled in the flying time was dealer's choice. My reaction, I'd imagine, was typical. At a discreet distance from the airfield, I ducked down to treetop height and had the time of my low-flying life; screaming up gullies, along country roads, pulling up and over high tension cables way too close to make any sense. The price was all lined up and waiting.

Once, when a strange castle perched high on a cliff loomed up ominously in front of me, and a line of mountains unexpectedly edged in on my world, mild suspicion started to cloud the fun. I pulled the stick back into my stomach, gave both throttles full bore, and shot up to five thousand feet. No doubt about it, the countryside was very beautiful, sun-drenched and soothingly tranquil. There was only one snag. It wasn't my countryside. Try as I might, I couldn't find anything in the bewildering scene down there to match the images on my nice new map. I was lost, utterly and completely.

What I did find down there, though, was this strange airfield, its concrete dispersal pans filled with Spitfire fighter aircraft. Obviously, it was time to stop playing king of the airways. Swallowing my pride, I slunk down onto their runway, admitting I had flown off my map area. I found that I was twenty-three miles south-west of my home base. The smiling strangers gave me a course to steer, apparently making no report to anyone about my unauthorised visit. Nor did I. And so it came to pass that no record of this error was ever made in my log-book.

In the middle of the fun, while these heady, free-wheeling days frittered away, no one really noticed as we went belting through that most important door marked "Never More". Somehow the reality didn't quite register as we frolicked around those summer skies, and chased hares zig-zag fashion along the runway with our Oxfords. But, like it or not, our fly-for-yourself days were over. From this point forward we would each be hooked up to a crew, responsible for their welfare as well as our own. As a crew we would fly together, socialise together, eat together, and, if the ball rolled the wrong way, die together.

The Wellington Bomber had started off its war as a front-line machine, one of Bomber Command's big names. True, its glory days were brief, the soon-to-emerge four-engine planes edging Vickers' product on to the sidelines. Nevertheless, this twin-engine heavy bomber had performed with distinction, spearheading the Allies' fight back to air supremacy in the skies over Europe. Its legendary feature was the amount of punishment it could absorb before falling out of the sky. Held together by the criss-cross web of geodetic construction, the Wellington could sustain sizeable flak holes punched out of its superstructure and still stagger on tenaciously to its home base. This, then, was the plane awaiting us at No 85 Operational Training Unit (OTU), Husbands Bosworth. At this new airfield was a veritable army of strangers in a variety of aircrew categories.

All categories would have a few days to mix in together in the mess halls, lecture rooms and walkways. During that time, they could group themselves into crews of six: pilot, navigator, bomb aimer, wireless operator, and two gunners — one rear, and one mid-upper. It was a democratic opportunity to link-up with the crew of your choice. The pilot was responsible for handing over the crew list to the flight commander. If, at the end of the week he failed to find a team, authority would take over and simply form crews from the names left unattached.

The seventh member of each crew, the engineer, would join us at the heavy conversion unit, the final rung in the training ladder. At that point we would switch over from two to four engines, that future plane being a Stirling, Halifax, or — hopefully — the Lancaster.

By the third day I had found two gunners and a wireless operator. By the fifth day the crew was complete for the time being.

At this point our crew list read as follows: Pilot, Philip Gray; Navigator, "Red" Greer; Wireless Operator, Harry Jenkinson; Bomb Aimer, Ken Luft; Mid-upper Gunner, Ivor "Blondie" Foster; Rear Gunner, Clinton Booth.

"It's called 'Spit In The Ocean' and it goes like this."

The tutor was our Navigator, Red Greer. The game was poker, or at least one variation of poker. Red had already shown us how to fine-hone our poker skills in such offshoots as Baseball, One-Eyed Jacks, Deuces Wild, Seven Card and, of course, Stud and Draw. His repertoire seemed endless. My favourite was "Bugger the Expense", but at this particular session of the action it was Spit in the Ocean.

I could see that Red was very popular with the crew. His easygoing style, that beautiful New World nasal drawl, together with his obvious talents at the poker table; all these meant that he was in there like the sleeves in a vest. Equally impressive, I may add, were his talents at the bar. After three triple whiskys, he stood there as clear-eyed and normal as if they had been glasses of coke. As his pilot, I could only hope his ability to navigate a heavy bomber through the murky night skies matched his abilities at the card table.

Ken Luft, the Bomb Aimer, was the one proving to be a bit of a puzzle. He was quiet and withdrawn to the point where it was almost embarrassing. If we were to function as a working unit, then Ken would have to come in a bit closer, both in the air and on the ground.

The Wellington was much bigger and heavier than anything I had ever flown. The cockpit check was extensive, the fuel system quite involved, and on top of all this, I was having no end of trouble getting the bloody thing back onto the ground again. I was highly sensitive to having anyone looking over my shoulder. Unfortunately, that's the only possible way to convert to a new type of heavy aircraft; an instructor has to ride shotgun in the seat beside the pilot. My temperament rebelled against it then, and still does to this day.

As it stood at this point, I was the only dumpling putting his credibility and skills on the line. The other members of the crew had just climbed aboard for the ride. And no doubt, as I struggled and all but sweated blood to get this Wellington act into gear, doubts must have been rippling through the ranks of my crew.

Luckily, I got things together before the chiefs ran out of patience. Now, with the entry "First Solo on Type" firmly wedged into my log-book, it was my turn to look over a few shoulders.

Practice for the Navigator and Wireless Operator was limited on these close-to-home fighter affairs. Flying to incorporate the Air Bomber, Ken Luft, was not possible at all. He had failed to report back from a weekend pass. An interview with the Flight Commander, flanked by the Bombing Leader, quickly revealed the problem.

"You are being assigned a new air bomber, Sergeant," explained the boss. "His name is Flying Officer Marner. My bombing leader assures me he is good at his business."

"And Luft, Sir?" I queried.

"Luft, I'm afraid, is having medical problems."

"I'm sorry to hear that, Sir," I replied, and sorry I really was.

Ken had been a quiet, well-mannered, refined sort of chap; maybe just a bit too refined for this ruthless business.

Our crew list had now altered to: Pilot, Philip Gray; Navigator, Red Greer; Wireless Operator, Harry Jenkinson; Bomb Aimer, Jack Marner; Mid-upper Gunner, Ivor "Blondie" Foster; Rear Gunner, Clinton Booth.

CHAPTER
TWO

The Heavy Stuff

Flights now would have the gunners using live ammunition on a drogue they themselves had released, or they would try to capture the image of an "attacking" fighter on film. There is no mid-upper gun turret on a Wellington, so Ivor, our crew member destined to fill that space, had to make do from the rear gun turret. The air bomber, in addition to the duty of releasing 25-pound practice bombs on the various bombing ranges, would also cut loose with his twin 0.303 machine guns from the front gun turret. Red would work on the navigation part, while Harry handled his radio equipment.

As the days rolled by though, and the cross-country flights became more ambitious, a real problem was creeping up. Red's navigation and logs were causing grief. At first the chiefs suggested the trouble might lie with my flying, a perfectly reasonable possibility, so on our next flight a Company pilot and a Company navigator climbed aboard to ride shotgun. The truth became clear. Red was taken off flying, given extra periods of ground training, and eventually handed back to us for a do-or-die effort to stay in the game. Two five-hour cross-country flights later, despite some of my most accurate flying, the axe fell. The Flight Commander called me into his office and told me that Navigation was sending Red back to Canada.

The news that we had lost Red was a bitter blow. He had become a real friend.

Next day the two gunners came along with another navigator they had been chatting up. His name was Gerald Merrick, and I'd say his age would give the rest of us about ten years, he registering about 31 years to our 21. What we didn't appreciate at the time was that we had just secured one of the best navigators in the business.

Right from his first cross-country, Gerry was shown no mercy by the weather. There seemed to be cumulus clouds permanently standing guard in our skies. These are colossal cloud structures that can reach from almost ground level up to 30,000 feet, with all sorts of permutations in between. These meteorological hazards are products of the summer months, or when the sun has warmed up the land surfaces. A plane blundering into one of these clouds can get caught astride the up and down currents. That would be the point where the plane could get bent, and the people inside would wish they hadn't joined aircrew.

Although Gerry was not too familiar with the Wellington machine, let alone his new crew, the cumulus monstrosities had no plans to back away. It was uncanny. No matter which course we chose, a bevy of these climatic calamities was there before us. This meant that we resorted to wild variations of course to side-step the source of aggravation. It also meant that Gerry had to work like hell to accommodate such quick-fire manoeuvres.

This happened many times during the mind-crushing introduction he had to our flying schedule, and yet not once did Gerry ever waver. On the contrary, the new course to steer came at me right on cue every time, his logs at the end of the day being beautifully printed, beautifully presented, and — most important of all — deadly accurate. Truly, the ball was beginning to run in our favour, crew-wise; we had the makings of a great team.

This seemed to be the case both when we were flying around the sky and fooling around on the ground.

Our crew list now read as follows: Pilot, Philip Gray; Navigator, Gerald Merrick; Bomber, Jack Marner; Wireless Operator, Harry Jenkinson; Mid-upper Gunner, Ivor "Blondie" Foster; Rear Gunner, Clinton Booth.

"Unless I'm losing the place, that bloody kite on the approach is on fire."

The explosive remark was Clin's. All heads swivelled around towards the threshold of Runway One Six. No doubt about it, the Wellington on the home run was belching smoke from the forward part of its superstucture.

"There go the heat and meat wagons," advised our ever alert wireless operator as fire trucks and ambulance took off from their stations like scalded cats, all heading for the touch-down point on the concrete.

We learned later that the plane was Z-Zebra, and that someone inside had used the Verey pistol while flying over base. Unfortunately, the cowboy firing the pistol had failed to clear the side window, causing the brightly coloured blazing identification cartridge to fall back into the cabin. On quick assessment, the pilot had chosen to go for a landing, though apparently the crew were readying to hit their parachutes.

The fact that the Wellington was a pussycat on night flying details helped only to a certain point. Catch someone at the end of two gruelling cross-country raids — say one day and one night — and then see what could happen. Flying Officer Gorman had carried out just such a stint; had run himself ragged, and was plain out of steam when he reached the home stretch. Most of us knew this territory very well, but he was too tired to care. He misjudged the final touchdown, bouncing his plane, T-Tare, so badly that one of the tyres burst on impact. This sent the luckless aircraft into a vicious ground loop, the speed still way too high. The Wellington pirouetted so many times, the crew must have thought they were on a rollercoaster ride to hell; so many times, in fact, that the plane wrote itself off. Happily, no one was injured. There was no fire.

The pressure was building up.

Our crew seemed to have little ole good fortune right in our pockets. We knew there was only one way out of this circus and that was by holding on as firmly as possible to the hand of our sponsor, Lady Luck. In our case, the proof was sprawled all over the record cards.

Next was the cumulus affair. Right up to the notorious six-hour long Raid 92/15, we had given these giant cloud formations the fingers. Finally we were caught while skidding along the second leg of that respected cross-country, when a boomer of a cumulus cloud straddled flush across our flight line. This time the fancy footwork got us nowhere, no matter how hard we tried, and we really tried.

After veering way over to starboard to go around on the right, and then swinging an agonisingly long way back to port to have a go at the route on the left, the truth finally got through. Big Cu had us cold! There seemed to be huge cumulus clouds everywhere. Moving from 14,000 feet to 18,000 was another loser. Looking upward from the astrodome, Harry reckoned this monster went up another 18,000 feet. High ground and strong currents cancelled out ideas of sliding underneath. Even behind us the shutters were coming down. The layer clouds back there were starting to ice up the plane's wingtips and leading edges, its propellers, the tail unit, and even the windscreen. We were in trouble.

Jack, occupying the spare seat behind the other set of flying controls and monitoring this circus, turned his head ever so slowly in my direction and offered a knowing, sympathetic smile. Neither of us said a word, both aware of the inevitable. There was only one way out, the final option, and that was to bore through the middle of our very first full-blown cumulus cloud.

I shuddered when I thought of the navigational manipulating Gerry must be sweating through to keep up with all of this buggering around.

"Sorry about this, Gerry," I had finally to admit over the intercom, "but can you please give me a course to make good the original flight line. Everyone else back there had better hold on to their back teeth. We are about to do a Geronimo through the middle of that bloody great Mama in front of us."

The navigation department was as sharp as ever.

"Course to steer, Skip, is 082 degrees compass."

As we surged towards the black canyons of this ominous cloud, my grip on the wheel atop the control column was vice tight, knuckles white, and the palms of both hands slippery with sweat. This current-riddled, much-feared titan gave us a ride to remember. For a time the only control I had was the right to admit that I had no control at all. Later I would admit that the experience did not match the battering I had expected from the potential of this 25,000- to 30,000-foot monolith. We were lucky!

Another day, returning from a mock bombing raid, we ran smack through the main bomber stream heading for Germany. There were Lancasters and Halifaxes whipping under and over us, and even zipping past us at our height. This was no place for amateurs like us. The crews in the bomber stream must have got the shock of their lives.

CHAPTER
THREE

The Promised Land . . . At Last

After messing around on leave, attending an aircrew school to make us more cohesive as a fighting unit and a battle course for no particular reason at all, we were then shuttled on to a place called Wratting Common in Cambridgeshire. This is the record of one minute incident created along the curiously off-beat path aircrew types were required to tread.

Over a period of two months we were shuttled from Husbands Bosworth in Leicestershire to Stradishall in Suffolk to Wratting Common, to Shepherds Grove in Suffolk, and back to Wratting Common.

Here, authority had decreed that a group of Women's Auxiliary Air Force (WAAF) personnel would vacate their Nissen hut to make way for the incoming aircrews. As we were to find out, the ladies were not about to accept this arbitrary heave-ho without registering the appropriate protest. They were to provide us with a sting in the tail.

We had been hoping, starry-eyed, to meet the Queen of the Jungle, the Lancaster. Instead, we were being fobbed off with yesterday's child, the slow and cumbersome Stirling bomber. Tired and not a little despondent, we trundled back to the Nissen hut we had been allocated, pre-occupied with our blighted hopes. There we would all flop onto our beds and wallow in our frustration and self-pity.

There was no doubt in our guilty little minds that the living quarters we had inherited had been made available at the expense of our WAAF compatriots. Everything was clean and orderly. Windows were spotless, carpets were at the doors, provision had been made to hang pictures on the walls, and the floor was polished to perfection. Obviously the place had been in the care of a higher form of life.

True to form, when the boys had left our previous home they had done so with a fair stock of tinned fruit and other assorted provisions in tow. The drill, as always, was to get the pot-bellied stoves in the Nissen hut fired up. Once they reached a red glow, the sliced Spam could be cooked to taste. Busy as little beavers, we had stuffed the paper into the gaping mouths of the fireplaces, and piled the wood and coke on top. Now all we had to do was light the fire and relax. At this point, our world fell apart.

No sooner had combustion got under way than smoke poured out of every crack and cranny around the stoves. The whole room quickly filled with thick, choking smoke. We were forced to evacuate the place, coughing and spluttering.

There was every possibility the previous lady tenants of the hut were monitoring this comedy from a safe distance, doubling up with laughter as they did so.

It was quite some time before we could venture back into our new home. As the smoke cleared and the fires were emptied out, we soon discovered the reason for the backfire action.

Each chimney was stuffed from bottom to top with sanitary towels — used sanitary towels. No smoke could trickle up these flues until every single towel had been removed from the pipes. This proved to be a long, weary, rather unsavoury job, one that had to be tackled from both inside the Nissen hut and the roof outside. The language was heavy and basic throughout this chore.

The thought festering away in the ladies' minds must have been, "Right! If these aircrew sods are going to move into our beautifully manicured home, they will pay for the privilege." Who could blame them? If aircrew were the blue-eyed boys, then make those blue eyes water a little from time-to-time. We suffered, but we understood.

It was much, much later in the evening before we enjoyed our feast of tinned Spam. By that time the black thought of Stirling bombers had soothed down quite a bit.

Next day, lectures on these aircraft began, running up to two-and-a-half hours in length. Eventually all of our knowledge was put to the test with a three-hour long examination. Oddly enough, there was never any suggestion that we be required to climb into a Stirling and actually fly one around the sky. Then came the heavy rumour that we were about to make another move, this time to an airfield called Woolfox Lodge where, the grapevine assured us, the owners had nothing but Lancasters. No one ever explained why we were being put through an examination on all aspects of the Stirling bomber if we were about to be transferred to a Lancaster base.

Sure enough, at Woolfox there were Lancaster aircraft on concrete dispersal pans all over the place. With not a Stirling in sight, all the information we had so carefully acquired could be flushed down the tubes. We would now have to start the tuition comedy all over again for Lancasters.

Not that we really cared any more.

Having been joined by an engineer at Woolfox Lodge, our complement of crew members was complete. The crew list now read: Pilot, Philip Gray; Navigator, Gerald Merrick; Wireless Operator, Harry Jenkinson; Air Bomber, Jack Marner; Engineer, Frank Parkhouse; Mid-upper Gunner, Ivor "Blondie" Foster; Rear Gunner, Clinton Booth.

CHAPTER
FOUR

Anyone Got A Corkscrew?

"What are you smiling at, Phil?"

Jack was asking the question as he walked toward me across the flight room. I was on my own in the corner, staring out at a group of technicians replacing an engine in one of the aircraft. Before I could orient and explain, Frank cut in from his seat by the table.

"Easy answer, Jack. Here we have a character who's now soloed the mighty Lancaster by day and by night. He's got every reason to smile. Right, Skip?"

"Good try," I agreed, "but you're wrong, Frank. That smile was echoing back from something that happened about a hundred years ago. A guy named Jack Evans shared a bell tent with seven of us at this toughening-up camp. The place was Ludlow, and Jack, a rear gunner, was having a torrid affair in town with a city official's daughter. Both of them were tigers. My smile was remembering his story about one of their sessions, told when he got back to the tent one night."

"Somehow, the way Jack Evans told the story it was really hilarious, especially when he came to the part where the maiden would be eating fish and chips while the love-making was still in progress."

"Anyhow, as the months piled on top of one another, I made another good friend at Calveley aerodrome while flying Oxfords. He was a pilot named Jim Hall, and, wouldn't you know, he ended up with Jack Evans as one of his gunners. Now we come to the black bit."

"One of the boys in the new crew who arrived here at Woolfox yesterday knew them both well. He also knew that Jim Hall and his crew were in a Lancaster that blew up near Peterborough about a month ago. They all got the hammer. Wherever he is, I bet Jack is still smiling as he ponders his outrageous love life."

Around me, no one at all was smiling as I finished the story.

"Let's do some flying," I suggested, trying to drag us all back to the here and now. I could see Flight Lieutenant Smith beckoning to me from his office. He was beaming like a dog with two bones.

"It's fun time, Amigo," Smudger winked at me. "Let's go do some fighter affiliation."

I smiled, he smiled, both of us mischievously aware that we would probably be the only ones on board enjoying the whole affair. No one could question the need for such an exercise.

Both bombers and fighters were aware of the strengths and weaknesses of the other, and both were continually learning new tricks and manoeuvres to lengthen the odds in their respective favours. The much larger and bulkier four-engine frame could never hope to match the fast, quick-changing, rapier thrusts of the "single engine".

The battle went on, and the corkscrew was one of the tools used by the bombers in that battle.

Every effort was made to ensure that one lone bomber would not be singled out by the fighters. Like wolves, the big planes travelled in packs.

There were many reasons why a bomber might find itself facing up to a fighter one-on-one: panic; being hit by flak; a fire on board or in one of the engines; losing the power in one or more of the engines; or straying off course while on a night target. The tension was always there, wise crews forever on their guard. All it needed to sow the seeds of doubt was a vague, unfamiliar shadow ghosting through the gloom.

Smudger Smith was about to initiate us into the all-action manoeuvre called the corkscrew, as it applied to the Lancaster. The Hurricane fighter detailed to "attack" us, made contact on the radio, sending Smudger straight into his patter.

"The big deal about this corkscrewing caper is to keep it simple and — never forget this one — make every move a move to the limit. Don't piss around. This isn't just another practice run at steep turns. When you get some real enemy fighters up your chuff, they won't hang around while you fill your pants. The one distressing thought in their depraved little minds is to blow you and your plane right out of the bloody sky. So, when you say 'down port', it means just that: stick hard forward for the dive, left foot hard in on the rudder, wheel fully over to the left — and then hang on."

"I'll go through the first one with you. After that, you're on your own. If you possibly can, always warn the crew that you are about to corkscrew, and keep chattering out a continuous commentary over the intercom, explaining exactly what you are doing. The crew might not like it, but at least they will know where they are going and why they are suffering."

Contact was made with the Hurricane to let the pilot know it was a go, and he could attack. Our upper and rear gun turrets were fitted with cine cameras to record any "hits" Blondie and Clin might make.

The fighter, which had been hanging about 1,000 feet above us, moved in to attack. Over the intercom, Smudger started the patter for the corkscrew, he and I with our hands on a set of the dual controls, although I was merely following through.

"Corkscrew! Corkscrew! Now . . ."

"Down port."

"Rolling."

"Down starboard."

"Rolling."

"Up port."

"Rolling."

"Up starboard."

"Repeat and repeat."

"About here, Fritz is beginning to sus the pattern — so change it."

"Down port."

"Rolling."

"Up starboard."

"Rolling."

"And so on, and so on . . ."

"Vary the corkscrew any way you wish, but always try to balance out the 'ports' with the 'starboards'. That way you maintain your original heading — roughly. Sure you'll be giving your crew a hard time, but then you'll be giving the bastard in that fighter a hard time too, and that's the object. Better to lose your breakfast than your life."

"By the way, if you ever get a comedian in one of those Hurricanes showing off with a couple of slow rolls, and then inviting you to do the same, there's only one thing to do. Stop one of your engines. Invite him to stop one of his. That'll piss on his chips." Smudger always did have a delicate turn of phrase.

We dropped Smudger off and carried on with the fighter affiliation assignment. Overall, corkscrewing was never a great favourite with the crew. As an evasive life-saving manoeuvre, in my opinion it was more effective by night than by day. Whatever the truth, it was a routine that made the fighters really work for their money, and there was always the chance that our gunners would get lucky. Then again, if the enemy fighters had the time and the patience, they did seem to have the dice loaded in their favour.

CHAPTER
FIVE

If We Can Get Away With This

Came the night of 19 December 1944. Other heavy days and nights would come and go, but this was to be the bitter, living end; the ultimate in misery, suspense, and nerve-tingling apprehension.

Two grief merchants, Trouble and Weather, were the culprits. These two worked one of the slickest double acts it had ever been my misfortune to sweat through. Neither one let a cue slip by. The drama got underway even before we left the deck, and continued on through the whole torment until we hit the concrete again about six agonising hours later.

Even back at the pre-flight briefing, the Meteorological Officer's diagrams had been bubbling over with warnings and bad omens. They were showing us a huge low pressure area standing guard over the whole of central and southern Britain. It had been sitting there so long, it should have been paying rent. The Met Officer forecast grim weather conditions at every point.

Trouble was to be the great deceiver — screwing up the rules — and there was no Trouble officer warning us at the briefing. When we expected the aggravation to come from that ominous black gloom on the horizon, instead it was sitting beside us in the cabin. Even getting into the air there was drama.

Our WAAF bus driver had to use all her muscle and know-how to keep the heavy vehicle on the perimeter track. All planes were parked on the outer fringes of the airfield, each up to one hundred yards from its neighbour.

As I watched the tiny rear light of her truck fading quickly into the gloom, I wasn't sure whether to feel sorry for her, or start running like hell in the opposite direction. Even to think about flying in garbage like this was suicidal. Luckily, we had a pal standing by.

Our Lancaster, M-Mike, did its level best to look proud and businesslike as we walked toward it, its huge reality the only friend we had in this night of madness. The poor thing was dripping with sleet and foreboding from tip to tail as seven reluctant aviators piled in through the side door.

Twice during the twenty-minute taxi run, as we probed and scrabbled to find the runway, I had to slither to a stop on that slippery perimeter track to allow Mike to build up brake pressure. At one point, during a heavy snow squall, I even wheeled our Lancaster into a parking-pan by mistake. Luckily it was empty, so I did a neat "wheely" around the huge concrete circle and returned to the perimeter track, restoring my self respect.

"Christ, this is more hilarious than a Keystone Cops comedy. We're dicing with death, and we're not even off the frigging deck." The observation came from Frank in the seat along from mine. I could only nod in agreement.

Finally, in merciful release, we thundered along the runway and melted into the anonymity of the night sky and the unknown. In the pitch black above, just as Buckingham had found out with his princes three hundred years before, we found no salvation. Indeed, it was the reverse. As we levelled off at 10,000 feet and covered the first two legs of the exercise, the weather grew progressively more hostile.

Seeing that garbage on the met charts in the briefing room was one thing; flying through the "actual" was something else again. On the fourth leg, at 21,000 feet, the temperature sagged to minus 47 degrees Celsius. It was so cold that even the cabin heaters were beginning to lose interest. It puzzled me how the Wireless Operator and the Navigator stayed in touch with reality in conditions like this. They were more remote from the heat flow than the other three crew members in the front cabin. The two gunners were wearing electrically wired suits. In their isolated gun turrets, all that stood between them and the full blast of the elements was the plexiglass of their revolving "outposts". To keep them warm, especially their trigger fingers, Ivor and Clin plugged their flying suits into the aircraft's electrical system.

Warm, that is, as long as the power kept flowing. A concerned call from Blondie on the intercom burst that bubble and broke in with the bad news. The power to his suit in the mid-upper turret had cut out, and he was slowly turning into a block of ice. Now, there was a situation. The easy option was to get Ivor down out of that turret, and into the front cabin to share our heater. On the other hand, that would be one fewer pair of eyes to probe for possible trouble in the snow-laden, sleet-flecked, dangerous gloom outside.

"Ivor, my boy," I answered to his radio call, "I'll lay it on the line. Up there you have the best view of all the action, and right now I need all the help I can get in that area. A shout from you in time might just save our necks. But, if you can't hack it, then come on down."

The radio fell silent for about five seconds, and then Blondie must have thrown his microphone switch to "send".

"OK, Skip, I'll hang on up here, but I'm warning you. If my balls freeze up and fall off before we get back, my girlfriend will never forgive you."

"That's fair warning," I said, smiling and happy that I still had a pair of eyes probing from the roof of the Lancaster.

A few seconds later we were hit with a fresh shower of snow, cancelling out everyone's night vision. If another aircraft had sliced across our track, the pair of us would have fireballed each other to infinity, long before either pilot could move a muscle. The snow effect was beautiful, soothing, and almost hypnotic. It was like flying towards deep space through an endless cloud of chopped-up cotton wool.

Varying heights and courses moved us over parts of the Atlantic Ocean, the North Sea, and chunks of England, but we saw none of this. The changing cloud patterns whipping past the identification lights on the wingtips were the outer limits of our world.

I tried to descend to a lower level, but was sent scurrying "upstairs" again by some very inhospitable medium cloud. The high altitudes held other "delights". In his rear turret, Clin could see ice starting to form on the tail unit. Where in hell was I supposed to turn to escape from this endless stream of bad news? Down we eased again, slipping below the unfriendly clouds, and losing the ice.

Twice during this five-and-a-half hour criss-cross of sea and land we passed directly over our home base, the two worlds separated by an impressive barrier of cloud, water, ice and lightning flashes. On both occasions the radio telephone voices were barely above a garbled static. Broken, echoing, far-away sounds mocked us from the earphones. Seven pairs of ears listened intently for a recall signal. None was forthcoming, at least not in any recognisable form. We were locked into this bitter comedy right to the last sick joke. In fact, we were so busy wallowing in our immediate problems that we completely failed to recognise the great deception itself.

Ice, endless impenetrable cloud, the bitter cold, snow, sleet, rain, electrical storms — all of these bogies were like the flamboyant gestures of the master conjurer. All were high profile and guaranteed to command maximum attention. Meanwhile, the real trickery was to come at us from a different angle entirely, but for now . . . we were still in the air; we were still flying.

In the final descent from 18,000 feet to the circuit height of 1,000 feet, I had to level off for a time at both

11,000 and 4,000 feet. Stabbing pains in Jack's inner ears were causing maximum discomfort, and he was suffering from periodic nosebleeds. I eased up on our plunge earthwards to afford him some relief.

When we finally cruised into the luxury of the circuit pattern, it was the best thing I had experienced since last Christmas. We could almost smell the bacon and eggs.

Then — perfidy and back-stabbing — came the final twist of the knife. Trouble, the real deceiver, sensing that five and a half hours of mental and physical punishment must have reduced the reluctant seven to jelly, was in there like the tongue in a boot.

As Frank selected "undercarriage down", the corresponding lights on the panel showed two greens to port, and one green and one red to starboard! There was something wrong. The starboard wheel was not fully locked down. Annoying, but it was no big deal at this stage. We applied the basic cures for the trouble: stretch the downwind leg and give one or two sudden upward jerks of the nose with the stick. Nothing changed! We overshot and applied the same cure with more vigour around each of the four legs of the circuit. The warning light stayed with us. There was a muttered oath from the very back of the plane. Clin could see nothing of this drama from his rear gun turret, but he had been listening to our patter on the radio.

"We've already been run ragged." There was real grievance in the voice. "What else are we supposed to prove?"

"Clin's right," said Frank. "We've had everything but the runway thrown at us tonight."

It was a second or two before he realised what he had said. By the time he looked along in my direction, I was smiling, admittedly in a half-baked, ironic sort of way.

"If we can't convince that stupid light to turn green," I said, "then they won't have to throw the runway at us, Frank. We'll have no alternative but to throw ourselves at it instead."

Eventually we let the Control Tower in on the secret. We were hanging above their heads with a sick undercarriage. Go back up to 2,000 feet, they suggested, and try some more dip and jerk, during which time we could all visualise the turmoil going on behind the honeyed tones of the controller.

Dive and jerk as we would, the lights on the panel remained the same.

"All right," said the boss, now on the radio himself, "fly low over the Tower, and we'll have a look at you from underneath here."

This was quite an unnerving exercise to carry through, considering all the things sticking up from an airfield. Still, it was the chief's idea, so, with everything hanging out — wheels and flaps — and the throttle back as far as manageable, I dipped Mike down from 1,000 feet on a nice easy glide over the Tower at about 100 feet. Approximately five varying strengths of light beam were focused on our underside as we swept by, the whole exercise not telling us anything much. After all, wheels hanging down there, whether locked or not, would still look just fine, but try to lean on them and they would fold up like a joiner's measuring rule.

Try hand pumping was the next order, and a successive number of arms and muscles pumped themselves to a standstill. Actually, we had already tried this one, but obeyed all the same. Just about here the uneasy shimmer of foreboding hit us. We held only one more major card. Play that, lose, and we were bust.

The Flight Commander gave the order: play the card. Blast the wheels down with compressed air! It was a decision both given and carried out with reluctance. We all knew that, once suffering the indignity of air for oil, the whole oil pressure system would have to be painstakingly bled to get rid of the last bubble of air.

Frank pulled the knob, actuating the hydraulic emergency gear. In "shocking" the oil out of the pipes, the hope was that the action would also shock the undercarriage into the fully locked "down" position.

Unbelievably, this draconian operation altered the situation not one tiny bit. There on the panel, almost with an air of defiance and glee, the same combination of lights stubbornly blinked out at us: two green to port, and one green and one red to starboard.

A moment's pause to digest the black tidings both in the air and at ground level, and then the very final sombre instructions issued from the headset. They sounded like the last rites.

"All except the Pilot and the Engineer, get in behind a convenient bulkhead. Cup your head in your arms, and then brace for the final run in."

Next came the advice to me, the Pilot, and I've an idea there was a fair dash of tongue-in-cheek mixed in there with the guidance. Oh, the advice was sound

87

enough, but it was high-powered, virtuoso stuff. The Flight Commander was aware that I was adequate at putting a Lancaster down in the dark with all things in my favour. Now he was calling on me to use Mike like some ballerina.

"Approach at minimum speed," he advised, "all anchors out. Place the good wheel gently onto the concrete, and quietly edge over onto the suspect wheel and undercarriage. If the dodgy set-up even starts to buckle, whip up the whole undercarriage, keep the plane grinding along straight, and get everyone out of there lightning fast when the Lanc comes to its shuddering stop. But, cheer up! It may not come to that at all. Just do the best landing you can."

Turning on to the final approach, I gave Control the routine "Finals" call and watched, mesmerised, as the outline of the runway started to come at me. I held the Lancaster rigidly in the two green lanes of the glide path indicators, all but sweating blood as the run continued, my hands slithering all over the wheel as perspiration oozed out of both palms. The traffic light indicators whipped past as we crossed the threshold, and I knew there was no more outside help. The floating sensation of feeling for that runway in the pitch dark was like easing onto an endless sea of eggs. I got the wild impression that the whole plane would just fall through the lot and we would never be seen again.

The wheels slid onto the runway in possibly the best night landing I had ever made in a Lancaster. A fresh sweep of adrenalin helped things along. The roll continued. I applied the brakes ever so gently, and

Mike came to a halt right in the middle of the runway, nose held high and businesslike as ever.

Nothing drastic had happened — nothing at all. I felt like shouting out: "Well done, Mike, you old bugger!"

Surprisingly, there was no panic to clear the runway. Apparently we were the only fools to complete the exercise that momentous night. All the other crews had jacked it in hours before.

Next morning the ground crew cut our whole pulse-stopping drama down to size. All boggle-eyed, we had bundled the questions at them. What had gone wrong? How did Mike manage to stay on its wheels? How close was the undercarriage to buckling? How did you manage to taxi the plane off the runway where we left it?

"Oh that," they said almost as a throw-away. "It was just an electrical fault."

"You're finished here, Jock. You and your crew are posted to 186 Squadron."

Flight Lieutenant Smith wheeled the statement straight at me in his traditional, non-smiling, "that's it" fashion. The item caught me flat-footed. Over the many weeks we had been at Woolfox Lodge, we had all grown accustomed to Smudger's take-it-or-leave-it approach to life, but this was a boomer. It came without warning.

Mid-morning the Tannoy system had announced that Flight Sergeant Gray was wanted at the Flight Office. That, I thought, could mean only one thing. Smudger wanted to discuss the caper we had gone through the night before, possibly filtering through the details step-by-step. Fair enough. So on the way over I thought up all the angles that might come up, sure that I had responses to cover our tails. Now the Flight Lieutenant and his announcement had brushed all of that aside, leaving me struggling for a come-back.

"Does that mean the whole course is moving out then, Sir?" I asked, more filling in with words than really taking part in any coherent conversation. I fully expected the reply to be in the affirmative. That had always been the routine in the past.

"Nope . . . just one crew . . . yours!"

Never one to engage in junk conversation, the Flight Commander must have noticed my jaw drop a couple of notches, and — way out of character — figured that maybe a little casual explanation wouldn't burst his boiler.

"The manner in which you and your crew handled the trauma of last night's six-hour riot from start to finish didn't pass unnoticed. The boss figured, and I agree with him, that if you could get away with that lot, then you could get away with anything. By the way, that navigator of yours is dynamite; I mean, he's really good. Believe it!"

"I'll say 'Amen' to that one, Sir," I replied.

"Good luck, chap," said Smudger, holding out his hand, catching my glance eyeball to eyeball. "Come back and see me before you go."

Bloody hell! The truth thumped in on top of my head: We're in! We're an operational crew!

I was trying my damnedest not to throw my hat into the air and give Smudger the double thumbs up. Now to spread the earth-shattering news to the six other members of this operational crew.

"Did you explain to the boss about that electrical fault, Phil? Last night's hiccup with the undercarriage had nothing to do with us." This from Frank who may have imagined that, as engineer, he could have been linked up with that part of our wild night.

"Wasn't even mentioned, Frank," I assured him.

Pause.

"Then what the hell did he want?" persisted an ever-curious Blondie.

"Don't tell me," chirped in Harry. "We've got to do last night's fiasco all over again?"

Smiling, I let things hang in the air for a few seconds before dropping the awesome news.

"There were accolades for us right down the line for last night's exercise, Harry. No, it was only a minor matter Smudge wanted to discuss: merely to tell me we've been posted to an Ops squadron — Number 186, Stradishall."

Ever so slowly the truth dawned on all of us, but Clin was the one who said it out loud.

"Bugger me, we're in the front line. Next time we get into the air, some evil bastard could be trying to kill us."

It was time to move on.

CHAPTER
SIX

A Shoulder In Time

It was such a circumstantial, fragile, momentary affair. There we were, Margaret and I, zeroing in on each other for what was to be little more than a glancing moment, a sharing of secrets, and then we were swirled away in the mindless confusion of war. Somehow it was a meeting that deserved so much more.

The pair of us met at this dance in an All Services Club in Cambridge; not in the usual may-I-have-this-dance, do-you-come-here-often, rubbish but quite accidentally at the sandwich counter. Margaret had bundled two cakes and a ham sandwich onto a plate, decided to help things along with a Guinness, and then hit monetary troubles. Oh, she had the cash all right. The trouble was, she had too much cash. She produced a fiver, and the system just couldn't cope at that particular moment. Margaret's perplexed glance met mine. I paid the girl behind the counter for both of us, and Margaret and I found a table, quite amused at what was, in reality, just a piece of trivia.

"I'll pay you back," she promised.

"That seems reasonable," I agreed, "but let's do it our way. Say you pay by granting me the privilege of the next slow foxtrot."

"Done," she said, flicking some stray locks into place, smiling as she did so.

"By the way," she added, "my name is Margaret Harrison."

Two dances later, and half-way through a drink, I became aware of Margaret's probing, questioning look.

"Where do you fit into this war, Philip?" she asked. "And before you answer, I can assure you that I'm on your side. I, too, am in one of the Services."

We both laughed at that one, because Margaret was one of the few people in the place out of uniform. Posters everywhere told us not to share our secrets with strangers. Margaret had read the placards too. Without waiting for an answer to her original question, she continued.

"I'm in the Wrens [Women's Royal Naval Reserve], and I've been coming in here for the past three months, on and off. The people at the check-in know me very well. Happy?"

She backed up her assurance with a pay book and a smile that could have started a war on its own.

"Ma'am, your integrity was never in doubt," I assured her. "I'm about to join a bomber squadron and, just in case you should ask, I am a bit apprehensive about the whole affair."

Margaret showed surprise.

"Now there's a coincidence," she said, leaning back in her chair, "because I'm in a similar situation. I, too, am about to join a high-powered signals unit down in the London area, and I can assure you I'm more than a little apprehensive at that thought."

"Then why spend three months in Cambridge?" I asked.

"The training unit is up here," she explained.

In behind all of the dances, all the banter, a blind man on his second bottle of whisky would have spotted it by this time. This maiden was no product of the nine-to-five, council flats fraternity. From the exquisitely cut burgundy suit, silk blouse, real nylons, and high-fashion leather shoes, there had to be connections in the right places to put this lot together during such times of austerity. The demeanour, too, came bubbling through with oodles of self-assurance, seeming to belie the fact that what we had here was a rather shy girl.

"Where's your crew?" she asked.

"Oh, they're spread all over Cambridge. The Rear Gunner and Wireless Operator left here earlier in the evening. They all know there's no great hurry to roll on. We have forty-eight hours to reach the Squadron, and that doesn't include today."

It must have been at least four dances later before Margaret asked the question, and I could sense that, self-assured or not, she had marshalled a fair bit of courage before doing so. It was no quick-fire, easy decision.

"May I ask if you would care to come to my place for a cup of coffee? And before you answer, I'll run that lot past you again. I said, 'Come to my place for a cup of coffee', not another beer."

The warning was fair enough, but it was quite unnecessary.

"Margaret, I'd be honoured to accept your invitation just exactly as given — for a cup of coffee."

We left the club, and the bond was already in place. After three months of intensive training, the lady was about to lay her credibility on the line in the Metropolis. My crew and I were about to get mixed up in a shooting war. We were both unsure.

Margaret's flat was the perfect place to lean on a shoulder. It was quite luxurious and equipped with all the bits and bobs which affluence could provide. The subject was most certainly never discussed, but it was obvious that the finance bank-rolling this place was substantial, no doubt using the Service salary for tipping waiters.

The coffee and biscuits came and went, a record filled in the background, a hand slipped into another, a head leaned on a shoulder. I had the feeling that, in addition to the apprehension, both of us were just a wee bit scared about our immediate tomorrows, not at all sure how we would measure up in this part of our war.

If there was someone to hold on to in the here and now, that was just fine; preferably in a place where there was no crashing and banging; no ice, snow, or sleet; no new challenge to crack; no dangers lurking around every corner. All the pair of us wanted was to get lost in the warm, soft security of the other's arms and body. The rest of the world could go drop off the edge of a cliff if it liked.

After what seemed like a lifetime, I heard this question come mumbling and bubbling out of the fireglow somewhere.

"You still alive, Philip?"

"Yes, thank you," I assured her.

"It's getting early," Margaret suggested.

"You mean late."

"Well," she reasoned, "if you count nearly one o'clock in the morning as late, then it's late. I'll make some coffee," added the naked, shadowy figure, disappearing into the bathroom. I heard a shower springing to life.

As we held on tightly to each other in the foyer, somehow the world seemed a much nicer place; we had found that shoulder to lean on. Addresses were exchanged, each wishing the other astonishing good luck in their next big project of war, with a final smile and wave as I turned the corner of the street. But I'm sure we both held another truth in our heart of hearts.

Our moment had come and gone.

Two bus trips and four train rides later we were closing in on Operational Bomber Squadron number 186. With still a little time to burn, no one seemed in any great hurry to charge in through the front gate. The market town of Haverhill was the last haven on our path, giving us a chance to ponder in a small café on one side of the shopping area. It was the unlikeliest of places, but we were about to get an early introduction to action off stage at an operational airfield.

Jockeying for position around one of the bigger tables in the place, we spotted, and were spotted by, Squadron Leader Bass. A mild-mannered and quiet person, the Squadron Leader and his crew had been on the same course as our lot at Husbands Bosworth Operational Training Unit. Then he had been Flight Lieutenant Bass. He came over, smiled, and had a few words with us.

"I'll be your flight commander at Stradishall," he told us as he was leaving. "See you in the morning."

As a sort of afterthought, he stopped to elaborate, thinking perhaps that his presence in a café would be puzzling us, he here chomping cakes in the middle of the afternoon instead of helping to run the Squadron. Then again, our new leader may have decided that now was as good a time as any to nudge us towards the realities of Squadron life.

"I'll have to return to my table. You see, one of our planes crashed four days ago while trying to get back to the airfield from an Op. They didn't make it. The people I am with are the parents of one of the crew, who were all killed. We've just been to the funeral of their son."

He had a tinge of sadness in his voice, but otherwise he showed no outward sign of emotion. As he walked back to his table, the same thought must have been with us all. In this game of violence and sudden death in which we were about to engage, that could be any one of our wives or parents sitting over there in a couple of weeks' time.

Happy days!

CHAPTER
SEVEN

Home At Last

Quietly, almost without our noticing it, we had stepped through to the other side of the mirror. After all these weeks, months and years of push and shove, we had finally come home. Now we were members of an operational bomber squadron.

The performance was never off stage. Yet another kite had crashed short of the runway, its pilot trying in vain to nurse home a sick plane, one badly hacked about by exploding anti-aircraft shells two hours before. His effort was awesome and he had almost made it. All seven inside died. It was sobering stuff.

"We've been here for a mere twenty-four hours," observed a non-smiling Frank, "and already we've heard about seven people being buried and seven more getting the 'axe' just off the end of the runway. Christ almighty, you could develop a nervous twitch around here without even trying."

Fairly put, I thought, with a nice dash of humour thrown in, but I could see that no one was smiling. For the remainder of the day we were picking up all sorts of facts, figures, rumours and possessions as we moved along. Throughout Service careers, the battles with the

Stores Section were legendary. To replace a worn anything — tie, footwear, cap, battledress top — had meant endless struggles. Now, as if someone had waved a magic wand, the reality of an operational station opened all doors. I had my whole battledress uniform replaced and, when I tentatively suggested I could use a pair of leather flying gloves, I ended up with two pairs. We all received top quality sunglasses, but Gerry came in with the big prize.

As Navigator, timing in his work was vital so he was issued with, and had to sign for, a top-of-the-range Rolex chronometer. At the end of our operational stint, assuming we were still in business, Stores very definitely wanted that beautiful watch back. Then again, if Gerry returned from an operational flight missing one of his arms, they suggested, they would be willing to negotiate!

On the operational crew front, Number 186 Bomber Squadron comprised approximately half Australian personnel and half "The Rest". Our combination, of course, was a Scottish skipper and six Englishmen.

As the resident "hit" men at Stradishall, we were what they called "daylighters". Mostly, but not exclusively. If the "chop" rate of the night squadrons rose significantly, or the Command wanted to impress with bigger bomber fleets, then we would jump in and help; just as they would oblige if we needed help.

No squadron operated without a leader, and we had picked up some interesting information about ours. Wing Commander Giles was a Canadian, and as tough and rugged as they came. Around six-foot-four and built like a rugby prop, he was regularly on the Battle Order. Formality, we were told, was not his bag. Once, when the Station Group Captain had tried to edge in some good old-fashioned "bull", Wing Commander Giles had laid it on the line. By all means, he had conceded, there was always the choice. Either there could be bullshit or there could be operational flying but, of course, there certainly could not be both. The Group Captain had phased out the "spit and polish" very rapidly, only too well aware of the consequences if word of enforcing it had boomeranged back to Head Office. Sir Arthur Harris, boss of the whole Command, would have carved the Group Captain's career up into little pieces.

"Bomber" Harris was truly a legend among legends, a man among men, his name etched in honour across the annals of anybody's warfare. He knew that in a successful bombing campaign there could never be half measures. Until the enemy capitulates, its cities must be pounded right into the ground.

Harris was revered by his personnel throughout the Command. If he had put out the word, his squadrons would have flown up to and through the gates of Hell. What stopped us in our tracks was the speed at which he was asking our crew to ride up to one of those gates.

Gossiping through the findings and happenings of the day, we had barely noticed a sombre-faced Clin come into the room, plonk himself on his bed, and start to unlace his boots.

"You look as if someone has stolen your lollipop," joked Harry.

"Not my lollipop," said Clin. "They stole my breath away. I just passed the noticeboard on the way here. We're on tomorrow's Battle Order."

"Tomorrow!" Frankie exploded. "Frig me, they don't waste much time around here, do they? We've only been here one day."

Things did seem to be moving a bit fast. Somehow I had expected a chatter with someone on the business of operational flying: how to filter into a bomber stream; how to stay out of trouble in the night sky; and maybe one or two tips on how to stay alive. As I shot into the Flight Office to check things out, there was a knowing smile on the Flight Commander's face. It was almost as if Squadron Leader Bass had been waiting for me to appear.

"Ignore the Battle Order." he said. "You and your crew leave tomorrow for Feltwell to learn all there is to know about this new bombing-come-navigational aid, Gee-H. It's a sort of super radar. On each flight home from that airfield there will be Spitfires coming in to attack your bomber. That should keep both you and your gunners on your toes. Happy corkscrewing! See me when you get back."

This news brought some smooth to our war, and we prepared for a week at Feltwell in Norfolk.

Almost as a throw-away in a conversation I was having with a pilot in the Flight Office, he had mentioned that not all groups were sent over to Feltwell: "only selected crews". That was a puzzle. How did a crew become one of the select few?

In our case it couldn't have anything to do with the pilot, because I knew me very well. "Adequate" would be the word I would have used to describe myself, and I'm sure that would be the word on my record card. This was the safest way to see things. My very first instructor of all, Mr Lockridge, had passed on the warning: "When you start to think you're an ace, Amigo, you're dead."

One by one I thought about each member of the crew, hoping to find an answer to the puzzle. That was when I thought back to Woolfox Lodge and the meeting with Smudger Smith in his office. Only the two of us were present when he had thrown in the afterthought.

"That navigator of yours is dynamite."

Bull's-eye! Gerry was the answer. The glowing words on his record card had guaranteed we would be one of the selected crews. After all, Gee-H was primarily a piece of equipment for use by the navigator.

"Would you believe," Harry cut across all our thoughts, "they actually teach low flying at this place. Its official title is Number Three Low Flying School. The Gee-H stuff we're here for must be a sideline."

Frank saw the irony.

"We low fly unofficially," he said smiling, "and we can end up in all kinds of disciplinary grief. Here they do it for a living."

I remembered one of my cactus-high sweeps way out over a lonely part of the Arizona desert, and smiled. Pounding over the deck with practically no height at all showing on the altimeter, it was the horses I had noticed first. They seemed to be tethered and at the same time all saddled up. Curiously, too, they appeared to be quite alone. As I thundered past the animals in the Harvard aircraft, I swung the machine around the slight rise in the ground in a wide sweeping circle, the down wing just about cutting a groove in the sand. That was when I saw them stretched out compromisingly on the ground, the cowboy and the lady. By that time the sweep around was almost complete, and I was practically flying back down their throats.

The whole thing had happened so quickly, it would be difficult to say who was the more surprised, the lovers or the pilot. I could almost hear them screaming their anguished question to the desert around them: "Just where in hell does one go for privacy in these wide open empty spaces?" What more could I do but give them a wave and a smile as I shot on my way, hoping against hope that I hadn't taken everything off the boil.

"You're smiling," noticed Frankie from the seat beside me, "so you must have seen the joke."

"It was nothing really, Frank," I assured him. "Just a far-away memory from another time. Low flying can be fun now and again."

At other times, of course, it could be deadly. On our third day at Feltwell, yet another crew in a Lanc on one of the School exercises wrote their aircraft off while coming in to land. Either it was a very bad approach or a horrendous attempt at a landing.

"Jeez, these crashes just short of the runway are beginning to haunt us, aren't they?" The concern was

103

Clin's. "I want you to promise us, Phil," he continued, "that you'll take super care on all approaches. I don't want to end up fertilising some farmer's field in Suffolk."

We all laughed at the thought.

"These wipe-outs on the last mile home are really beginning to disturb you, Clin," I smiled. "Don't let them get to you, or you'll get the twitch every time we come in to land."

On the flight line at Feltwell the instructors got right down to business, quickly dispensing information on the new, very secret super radar called Gee-H.

The real fun for me came along on the way home from each Gee-H exercise. One of the very latest high-powered, clipped-wing Spitfires would zoom in on the attack to allow us to practise fighter evasion. The corkscrewing, on these occasions, was vicious stuff. Understandably, one or two in the crew were none too keen on this manoeuvre.

We returned to the Squadron at Stradishall, and, equipped with all this new knowledge, were now ready for operational flying.

CHAPTER
EIGHT

Through "The Gate"

Two nights later we were again back in business on the Battle Order for the next day. As the curtain over the blackboard in the briefing room was pulled aside, Wesel showed as our target for the second time. The inhabitants of that poor little township must have wished the war would just go away.

This second operational flight was to confront me with one of the most bizarre and frightening happenings that I have ever experienced in my life. Even now, half a century later, the very thought of this incident can speed up my pulse rate.

In the beginning, though, there was the briefing, and that was where I saw Judy for the first time. She was the officer giving out the intelligence angle: the strength of the defences we were liable to encounter; the reason for the attack; and, should we have to get out and walk, the best direction to succeed with the escape and evasion slant.

"I could be evasive with her any time she feels like it," Harry assured us in an undertone, his eyes never leaving the platform. "She can even have my whole chocolate ration."

The rest of us either had other things to think about, or we were keeping our desires to ourselves. I know I kept mine out of sight for the time being. Judy was a flying officer and I a flight sergeant, so look and admire was the highest aspiration on today's programme.

Judy's advice on escape and evasion was certainly interesting. Some aircrew carried revolvers or automatic pistols stuck down the side of their flying boots. I carried emergency rations in my left boot, the container shaped to fit the calf of my leg, and a folded rubber map of the country in my right boot. Being rubber, there would be no problem if I landed in a river or a lake. The map would still be usable. Even the flying boots could accommodate. If necessary, the top legging parts of the boots could be unzipped, leaving the wearer with a pair of shoes. We were all issued with magnetised metal trouser buttons which had a red dot on the rim. If balanced on the point of a pencil, nail, or twig, the red dot would always point to north.

The briefing for our second tactical target, Wesel, was completed. We had been wheeled out to the planes in the Company transport. I began slowly taxiing toward the start of the runway. For me, the real drama of this operational flight was now just a few minutes away.

The Aldis lamp from the runway caravan controller flashed green at our plane, R-Roger, signifying that it was clear for me to taxi the plane on to the threshold and line up for take-off. Radio crossfire was forbidden until we had gone through the target, thus denying the enemy any clues of our devious intentions.

While waiting for permission from the second and final green light to roll the Lancaster on its way, the four throttles were eased forward to zero boost (about two-thirds of our power), the brakes firmly locked to stop any forward movement, and the control column pulled right back against my stomach. All the engines were booming along just fine.

Curiously, at no time had I ever been tested in or taught the considerable art of lifting a fully laden Lancaster off the ground. This omission in my education was about to come very, very close to wiping us out, plus causing one bloody great explosion right there on the airfield. True, I had already got away with lifting a fully loaded bomber off the deck for the first Wesel raid, but luck must have been in my corner then. This time these four mighty Rolls-Royce Merlin engines would box me right into a corner. They would never get the chance to do that again. This time I would choose to use the full-blooded power start, right after releasing the brakes. I would never do that again.

So there R-Roger stood at the threshold of Runway 25, champing at the bit against the powerful hydraulic brakes, all four engines raring to go. The second green beam flashed across the space between the caravan and the plane, followed immediately by a hiss of relief as the pent-up hydraulic brake pressure made its escape into the atmosphere. From this point forward, everything was riding on those Merlin engines.

If one motor had cut on take-off, everything and everybody in our path would have had the most exciting two minutes of their lives, a fair part of the landscape being reshuffled in the process. On this occasion it was the sheer power of these Rolls-Royce units, together with their impressive three-blade propellers, that was to cause the excitement. Each engine stood at 3,000 revolutions per minute, the boost at 14 pounds per square inch, all four units each developing 1,400 horse power. That power transferred to the propellers — four sets of propellers spinning in the same direction — and the torque or pull of their blades immediately set up a strong swing to port.

It just so happens that with the bull's-rush type of take-off I had chosen, the pull to port was more pronounced and I found myself fighting this tendency straight away, promptly initiating the standard correctional measures. These called for hard right pedal to help the rudder convince the nose to come back into line, with full power on the two port engines while easing up on the power on the two starboard engines, again to help bring that nose back to centre line. All these measures together partly succeeded in normalising the situation. True, we were still sliding ever so slightly to port, but nothing too dramatic. The problem lay elsewhere. With these measures in place, the speed would not build up. The concrete was already disappearing fast behind us. Dramatic action was needed urgently.

We were now nearly half-way along the runway, still travelling at no more than 70 knots and gaining nothing. If we carried on like this we would plough off the end of the runway with the wheels still running along the ground. The situation called for at least 100 knots to safely ease this lot off the deck. Clearly the four Merlins, or should I say their propellers, were winning. Either I took off their way or they would bury us all.

I eased up on the right rudder, let the nose swing its merry way to port, and gave all four Merlins full power. R-Roger was now tearing across the grass, veering away from the runway, but the speed was building up very slowly — too slowly.

From this point forward I made up the rules as I went along. Obviously our exit from the field would be way off the normal flight path. Trees, telephone wires, and even high tension cables could be in the way. To clear these I had first to get the Lancaster off the ground, then whip up the undercarriage. Just as the wheels kissed off the grass, the plane turned slightly more to port. We were now seventy to seventy-five degrees off the original runway line.

Flush in line with our new take-off path was the biggest bloody hangar I had ever seen.

"Jesus Christ," blurted out a disbelieving Frank, "what the bloody hell do we do now?"

"Push everything through 'The Gate', Frank!" I ordered.

At normal maximum power for the take-off run, all four Merlin throttles are pushed fully forward right up to a stop bar called "The Gate". This is the top operating power necessary for almost every manoeuvre the Lancaster would ever have to complete. In an extreme emergency or as an operational combat necessity, The Gate could be raised, allowing the

109

throttles to be opened still further. Such action was murder on the Rolls-Royce units, and had a permissible time limit of only five minutes' use. Any longer than this and the punishment was liable to tear the engines apart.

I then got a shock from a most unexpected quarter.

"You've left it too late, Skip," was the Engineer's unbelievable reply.

I was flabbergasted. Frank had never hesitated like this before, and this was one helluva time to start.

"For frig's sake, Frank," I urged angrily, "push the throttles through the frigging Gate, NOW!"

At this stage in the drama I couldn't raise The Gate myself, push the throttle on through, juggle with the rudder pedals, and have both hands on the Lanc's steering wheel at the same time. Through The Gate went the four throttles! The engine note changed up to agony level. We were off the deck — just — and the Lancaster was thundering toward the hangar, the last of the grass screaming past beneath us. The closer we flew, the bigger the structure became.

I was calling on those Rolls-Royce power units to pull off a miracle. From barely above deck level, they had to lift 2,154 Imperial gallons of petrol, the seven of us, a 4,000-pound blockbuster, twelve 500-pound armour-piercing bombs, and the Lancaster itself over this colossal hurdle in their path.

With even the grass starting to run out of fashion, I could see we were still twenty to thirty feet short on height to clear that hangar roof. How I cursed those valuable seconds Frank had wasted earlier. At the very least, the poor old Lanc needed 150 knots to claw its way over the top. We were at 140 knots. My heart count must have been five thousand to the minute, and I was sure my adrenalin had vapourised long ago.

At the last possible, agonising moment, still looking up at the last part of the roof in front of us, I pulled the stick back, stared wide-eyed in front of me and simply held on. Only God Almighty Himself could sanction the success of this happening from that point. I was now just a passenger, my mind frozen into its own mental ice. One thing I know for sure: no part of my life passed before my eyes at this time, the nearest I had ever come to meeting my Maker so far.

According to a mesmerised, or was it terrified, Clin in the rear turret, the fully laden bomber actually sagged down the other side of the hangar after it staggered over the roof, steadied itself, and ever so slowly started to pull away. The four Merlins were still screaming for mercy at their extreme setting through The Gate. Luckily for us, our Lancaster held on to just enough height and speed to clear the trees and power lines filling the scene at the other side of the hangar.

Being still comparatively new to the Squadron, I was holding on to the old Training Command, cap-in-hand order of things. My first crazy thought, when normal thoughts started to squeeze through the cracks in the crisis, was that there would be hell to pay for this debacle when I got back to base. In reality, no one ever mentioned the happening; not the Flight Commander, not any of the other pilots or aircrews, not even my own crew. Probably, like me, their imaginations had stunned them into silence. If we had been short another two feet in height — and that I am sure was about the strength of our margin — then we would have pulverised that hangar into matchwood, our 10,000 pounds of high explosives powdering us across the nearby fields.

In a haze of suspended stupefaction, I took R-Roger from that hard-won, 100-foot life-savouring point to our bombing height of 20,500 feet to join the bomber stream. Up to and through the target storm, the old dangers, fears, and apprehensions came back. The flak was heavier this time, the Wehrmacht having apparently moved up some more anti-aircraft guns to protect itself. We saw a few of our bombers go down in our part of the action, but personally I am sure I was reflexing most of the time. I was insulated from the horrors around me over Wesel by the image of that even greater horror earlier on. I kept seeing that colossus rearing up in front of us like the New York skyline.

In the quiet of my thoughts, long after we had returned to Stradishall, I could see things as they truly were. We could go on from here for two more operational flights, or we could even brazen our way through a whole tour of operations; we could slide along the edge of doom in a thousand different ways, but that hangar episode was the clincher. My personal opinion was that whether on my own, or as a crew, none of us would ever be so close to the hammer again.

For me at least, everything — all of life itself beyond that hangar roof — would be a bonus. For once, that age-old cliché came right up to its full value and meaning. There, during those few fleeting moments, we had truly "diced with death" and got away with it.

Many years later there was a postscript to that infamous hangar roof affair. While discussing Stradishall and 186 Squadron with a lady — a member of the Women's Auxiliary Air Force at the time — I was told that, immediately after the incident had occurred, our death certificates were promptly prepared, one for each member of the crew. The person ordering the forms to be readied was her sergeant, the NCO in charge of the Administration Block at Stradishall. Apparently he had witnessed the hairy take-off and reasoned that it would be only a matter of time before the death certificates were required.

CHAPTER
NINE

Any Yank 'Drome Would Do

The blackboard in the main office of "B" Flight, 186 Squadron, was just about as ordinary as any I had ever seen. There were spaces provided for the names of approximately twenty pilots, followed along each line by further spaces for the names of the six other crew members. Each individual privileged to have his name chalked on that board had worked hard to get there, travelling a rocky, rugged road to reach this zenith in his flying career. Each was a volunteer, laying his head on the block practically every time he left the deck, hoping like hell that the axe wouldn't fall before he got back down again. But then, names are just names. The column that really carried the clout was way over on the right hand side.

This was the column headed "Ops. Completed", the one which clearly separated the "rabbits" from the seasoned operators. The one dicy, dangerous route to build up the prestigious total in this space was the highway through the shambles and devastation of an enemy target. It was while staring ruefully at our puny count of two operational flights, that I became aware of the Flight Commander standing alongside me. Our leader obviously knew what I was thinking.

"Give it time, Flight," Squadron Leader Bass suggested. "Your tally will soon shoot up the scale. We all had to start with a big zero in that space. Anyway, I have a message from the Adjutant. He wants you to zoom over to his office at 1000 hours to fill in forms 1020A. These are the bits of paper that will help put your commission into place. OK?"

"Yes, Sir," I assured the man whose name was right at the top of the blackboard. "The Adj's office at ten hundred."

"By the way," the boss half turned with an afterthought, "remind him about the 300 clothing coupons while you're over there. You'll need these when you get to the big city."

"Understood, Sir," I assured him.

I had half expected Squadron Leader Bass to slip in a casual remark about our second Wesel adventure, even if only in jest. There had been the nail-biting hangar drama on the way out, and then the crafty bit of diversion on the way back. We had been pushing our luck. Like the rest of us, the boss hadn't joined the Squadron yesterday. He knew the score.

If we had been able to reach a base a dozen miles from home, then surely a few more minutes in the air would have caused us no pain. After all, our Lancaster was scar free, with not a bullet hole or flak scud in sight. Probably our Flight Commander had his own thoughts, but was too much of a gentleman to indulge

115

in throw-away banter. He was already back behind his desk organizing tomorrow's escapade.

For months, almost from the time we had all hooked up as a crew, Ivor had niggled on about slipping into a Yankee 'drome. On the second return trip from Wesel, the Mid-upper got in one more plug for his cause.

"Weather looks rough down on the deck, Skip," his information filtered out of the earphones. "We may have to divert. Any American airfield would do."

I couldn't see it, but I could sense the mischievous smile that went along with the insistent suggestion.

"Hang in there, Blondie," I got back to him. "When the opportunity comes along, we'll be in there."

Starting from infinity way above us, and coming down through our descending height of 16,000 feet to approximately 5,000 feet below us, the weather was clear and sunny. The beautiful azure blue sky seemed to stretch on for ever. Following that heart-stopping hangar affair, and the disgust of the target, our serene and ever so gentle glide earthwards was like drifting quietly through some privileged wonderland in deep space. The warmth of the sun's rays coming in through the perspex was adding to the illusion.

The one ugly thought scarring its way through the tranquillity was the unpeaceful one of the enemy. We were still well within the range of their highly manoeuvrable fighter aircraft. If one or several Focke-Wulf 190s came beaming down out of the sun now, we would have one helluva job trying to lose 11,000 feet in time to escape their bullets and cannon shells. Our own fighter cover had cascaded down from

30,000 feet to deck level long ago, for all the world like a pack of schoolboys let out of the classroom half an hour ahead of time.

Blissfully, no enemy fighters broke the spell, and so placidity ruled on. But that fluffy, woolly-type cloud down at 5,000 feet was coming closer, ever closer. Like the blue skies above, the cloud cover below, too, seemed to stretch to infinity. From past harsh experience we knew only too well that, cosy and beautifully soft as this pure white carpet of water vapour appeared on top, its underside was usually a hell of low visibility and blinding rain. The cloud cover on this occasion, after the Wesel raid, was true to type.

After the peaceful life in the upper air, we reluctantly slid into the white cotton candy, its texture turning gradually from off-white to plain messy dark grey. My eyes were now glued to the instrument panel, especially the altimeter. At 500 feet we dropped through the bottom of the vapour blanket into a scene of desolation. From blue skies, sunshine and serenity, we were now flying through what seemed like semi-darkness, the rain falling steadily, adding to the misery.

"You were dead right, Ivor." I thought I had better acknowledge the fact. "The weather down here is a bastard. It's dangerous, too. Can everybody with a spare pair of eyes keep rubber necking all around us. There must be heavy bombers all around us, each one thundering home to its own haven. I'd hate to bounce off one at this height."

It was a situation our Mid-upper Gunner just couldn't — wouldn't — let slip away, his head in that

117

upper turret no doubt already bobbing in and out of the cloud base.

"Come on, Skip," Blondie came in almost on cue. "Let's have a go at a Yankee 'drome."

I gave a quick side glance at Frankie in his engineer's seat just along from me. He winked and smiled. I smiled at both his wink and Blondie's perseverance, my eyes back quickly and staring out once again at the dismal, dicey scene ahead. There was nothing wrong with the gunner's idea really, and we would probably never have a better excuse.

"What d'you think, Gerry?" I asked my Navigator over the RT. "Would it be fine with you if we did a side-step into a Yank airfield?"

My reason for singling out Gerry for the question was that, as navigator, he was the one to lose most face if we stopped short of our own base. It might look as if he couldn't get us home.

"Please yourself, Phil," Gerry said quite cheerily. "I don't mind. We could actually be home in about five minutes if you hang on to the course you're on now. Then again, if it will get our blonde-topped friend off your back, go for it."

"I heard that, Merrick," cut in the Mid-upper, his words laced with mock injury, "but I like your idea."

"Fair enough," I relented, "we'll have a go, but I hope you realise what this could cost me, Ivor. After leap-frogging that frigging hangar, and now lobbing into a Yank 'drome just about next door to home, our leaders could cancel my commission for ever."

"Turn about five degrees to starboard, Skip," Gerry cut in, "and you should pick up Sudbury."

"Thanks, Amigo," I replied, edging the Lancaster around a little to starboard. Three minutes more flying and the American airfield loomed out of the muck, Flying Fortresses parked all around its real estate. There was no aircraft movement of any kind.

"You there, Harry?" I enquired.

"Here, Skip," from the Wireless Operator.

"Bang off some reds with the Verey pistol while I do a wide safe circle around. If they come back with a green in answer to your reds, we're in."

Sure enough, following Harry's private fireworks display, a green light came beaming out at us from the flying Control Tower. I lined up R-Roger on a circuit that would use their longest runway. There didn't seem to be any appreciable wind. At long last Blondie had realised his dream. We were taxiing on American-controlled concrete.

Next morning the American Flight Commander asked if we would be interested in a flip around the countryside in one of his Fortresses. We quickly agreed, piled into the B-17, and had a good look around as the crew got us into the air. There were guns everywhere — nose guns, tail guns, mid-upper turret guns, two waist gun positions, one belly gun turret hanging underneath the plane. There must have been a crew of ten or eleven to cope with this rash of artillery.

The one point that staggered me, though, was the size of the bomb bay. It could accommodate only six 500-pounders at maximum load. To my way of thinking, truly, it just wasn't worth risking ten lives to drop six small bombs. This meant that it required four Flying Fortresses to deliver the same weight of high explosives as one Lancaster. Or put another way, about forty men would risk their necks to do what the Royal Air Force could achieve with seven.

As we prepared for take-off next morning in the now brilliant sunshine, there were US Army officers mingling all around the Lancaster, cameras capturing the image of a real bomber on their film. "Jeez, man," said one major, obviously impressed with the Lanc, "what you have here is one bloody great flying bomb bay."

After having enjoyed lots of generous American hospitality over the past few hours, it seemed prudent to say nothing at all in reply to that one. There was no point in denting Allied relations with any comparisons between the Lancaster and their bombers.

"Give them an old fashioned one, Skip," urged Clin as we taxied out to line up for take-off.

"Best idea I've heard today," I agreed. This called for me to hold the nose just a few feet off the deck, long after we were airborne and the wheels locked up. At runway's end, and it was one very long runway, back came the stick, and Roger rocketed into the wide blue yonder in style. I'm sure it must have looked good. It certainly felt good.

Back home at 186 Squadron, the action was about to move up a gear, all kinds of turmoil and adventure coming our way as the war rolled on.

PART THREE

THE PROFESSIONALS

CHAPTER
ONE

The New Breed

"It always sounds so easy, doesn't it, when they give out the griff from the platform."

Harry had made the point, his tone muted and somewhat deliberate. We were sitting next to each other in the briefing room waiting for proceedings to get under way. I could tell by the fixed stare on our Wireless Operator's face that he was talking as much to himself as he was to any particular one in the crew.

Indeed, no one came back with a reply, mute acknowledgement that all within earshot had agreed with his statement. It was waiting and wondering time in the spacious, cavernous room, pipe and cigarette smoke spiralling up to the ceiling, the banter and laughter sounding just a wee bit forced and artificial.

People were still filtering into the room; all levels of rank from sergeant to group captain; all classes of aircrew trade from air gunner, through navigator, wireless operator, and air bomber to pilot; much of their dress colourful and quite unofficial. All had a common knowledge. Once they had walked through that entrance way, they were committed, and there was one way only by which they could walk back out again.

Each one would have to go on a head-to-head with the chopping block one more time.

As the Wing Commander got to his feet, the chatter gradually tapered off to silence. All eyes were fixed — almost mesmerised — on the easel holding the target map for the day. At the moment it was covered with a cloth.

Wing Commander Giles flipped this back and exposed a city in a familiar part of the Third Reich. The target was Gelsenkirchen in the northern half of the notorious Ruhr Valley. For our crew, this was to be our first visit to the place. A month from now we would be on first name terms with the city.

"Gelsenkirchen, gentlemen, is like Father Christmas," our Canadian leader assured, starting the briefing in his easy, confident style. "It's got lots of goodies in its sack. Indeed, since day one of this rumble, Bomber Command has been over that city more times than you've had hot dinners. This time our target is a synthetic oil plant here on the east side. It's called . . ."

And so the detail unfolded.

Another detail had dawned on me not long after meeting our new boss. WingCo Giles was one of the new breed, as were all of the fresh crews coming along in the closing stages of this confrontation. Our head man was one of us. That's why he was such a popular leader. Time had changed the product.

Five long, long years ago, in a different world, Britain had gone to war equipped with a Territorial Army, an Auxiliary Air Force, and part-time Naval cadets. Aircrew, especially the pilots, had been recruited from university air squadrons, the more affluent homes in the land, and quite a few from the titled layer of British society. The free world, Britain included, had just survived a bitter economic depression, and these were the people trained and available when battle was joined.

The bravery and deeds of these flyers of 1939, 1940 and into 1941 is etched deep into the battle records of those early years. They were asked to front up to an enemy whose pilots and machines were battle hardened, and they were asked to do so in planes that were not quite up to the job. True, the Spitfires and Hurricanes were formidable fighting machines, but the Hampdens, Whitleys and Swordfish were in the wrong war.

These early years of World War Two exacted a terrible toll from both pilots and planes. Attrition had taken away many of the brave idealists who had swung all too readily into the cockpits of these inadequate chariots.

By 1942/43, the flight rooms of the Royal Air Force were witness to the arrival of a new breed of fighter. The idealists were being replaced by realists. Even the parlance and jargon of the day was changing. Wing Commander Giles and many of those facing him that morning would not have resorted to such expressions as "jolly good show", "what ho?", "pip pip", or "old boy". Such phraseology just wasn't their style.

Then again, while a style may change, the enemy remained the same.

The Navigation Leader was now on his feet.

"Let me take you through the routes and courses of this operation," he was offering. "And this, of course, is

125

mainly for captains of aircraft and air bombers. Navigators, as you well know, have already gone through all of this in much greater detail."

The route to any enemy target was always a fascinating, zig-zag, devious affair, and for good reasons. It must cause maximum confusion for the enemy, who could pick us up on their radar soon after we had left the English south coast. As the pilot map shows, the compass courses to and from a target give little indication of either its location or that of the home bases of the bombers.

Our 186 Squadron was a unit in Bomber Command's 3 Group, the only group equipped to bomb with Gee-H radar. The system was accurate and relatively easy to operate. Once in the air, the Navigator fed the target coordinates into his Gee-H radar set. With the bomb doors open for business over the target city, the Navigator could then release our little bundles of deadly joy from his navigation table. He need never actually see the target. In fact, Gerry, our very capable Navigator, once admitted to me that he never did see an enemy target. Lucky him! In reality, the Air Bomber was the one to drop most of the cargo from our aircraft.

For concentration of effort, we regularly flew in V-formations of three bombers, which meant that the lead bomber was also the Gee-H leader. When he dropped his bombs in compliance with the coordinates supplied, the air bombers in the Lancasters on either side of the lead machine would then release their loads of destruction when they saw the second bomb leave the leader's bomb bay. That was the basic plan, but, as

Robbie Burns had warned his contemporaries many years ago, the best laid basic plan can fall flat on its face at any time.

Once in the air, there were so many distractions. This time was no exception. Over Gelsenkirchen the anti-aircraft fire was heavy, accurate, and dead-on height.

"Christ, these ground gunners are good," our Rear Gunner had to admit, no doubt reluctantly.

"I should bloody well think so," plugged in the Mid-upper, no doubt equally reluctantly. "They've had years of practice."

Sweat was trickling down my back, my main concern of the moment being the Lancaster on my port side. Its pilot was flying starboard wingman to a Gee-H leader, and he was obviously more concerned with formation flying than safety flying. Our bomber and his were converging; very slowly, but converging nevertheless.

Ivor, too, had seen the danger from his mid-upper turret.

"Skip, you watching that gumball on th . . ."

"I'm watching him, Blondie."

"You'd think some frigger in his crew would warn the skipper."

A box of four ack-ack shells exploded just ahead of our three bombers. My reflexive evasive action to jump the aftermath of the explosions must have been just a wee bit too energetic. I had lost both the cohesion of the formation and my Gee-H leader. I was hanging above the other two bombers like a vulture about to strike. There was no time to regroup, so I elected to go in as a solo.

"We're on our own, men," I had to report to the Navigator and Air Bomber. "You'll have to drop our bombs."

"No problem, Phil." Gerry always sounded as if he were out for a stroll along a country lane. "Just hold the course you're on now."

"Wilco."

Despite the accuracy of the enemy shells, our gaggle of bombers was still intact. We had seen no one in our Squadron go down. From the rear turret, Clin had seen grief for a bomber behind us, spotted with one of its inner engines on fire. At this point even more of that basic plan was about to "gang a-gley".[1] While I — and no doubt all on board — was sweating out the expectation of flak, shards of shrapnel, or enemy fighters, it was the Navigator who brought the bad news.

"I've pressed the release button, Skip, but nothing has happened." He sounded annoyed.

"I'll have a go, Gerry." Jack jumped in before I could say a word. He was in the Air Bomber's front enclave, with the equipment to control the contents of the bomb bay. We were all poised for the dramatic uplift of the plane as the bombs were released. A Lancaster could gain 500 feet in height at this time, woofing upward like an express lift as its cargo fell earthward on its mission

---

[1] "The best laid schemes o mice an men gang aft a-gley." *To a Mouse*, Robert Burns, Nov 1786.

to rearrange the geography of the German landscape. Nothing happened.

"Sods won't go, Phil," Jack sounded even more annoyed than his Navigator, and not a little mystified. "I'll have to use the jettison bar. Hold on."

We had obviously overshot the aim point by this time. Courtesy of our Air Bomber, though, I had been educated about the jettison bar. The trick was to make very, very sure that the 500-pounders were dumped first, followed by the Cookie. The reverse order would be lethal. The 500-pounders would then bang into the Cookie, causing it to explode prematurely just under the tail of the bomber, vapourising the Lancaster and all who sailed in her.

Roger reared up in obvious relief, just as Jack brought us the good news.

"They're gone, Phil," the Air Bomber informed, "somewhere over the Ruhr. Couldn't have happened to a better place."

During all the time we flew together, I never once heard our Air Bomber resort to expletives, even when he was riding the razor's edge. Our Navigator, too, was in the same category. The rest of us, especially the Pilot, used all sorts of four-letter and multi-letter Anglo-Saxon additives to hide behind. At times these curse words were the only avenue of escape we had left. This colourful invective was definitely in the vocabulary of the new breed.

About thirty minutes short of base, I became aware of our Engineer staring intently, and apparently not a little puzzled, at my instrument panels. "If you've found something wrong over there, Frank," I looked at him quizzically, "do me a favour. Don't tell me about it."

Ignoring the flippancy, my companion on the flight deck was pointing to the top left centre of the dial array.

"That one," Frank was zeroing in on one of the dials with his index finger, "has always puzzled me. What's it for?"

"Oh that," my interest was waning. "That's the Direction Finding Indicator. If an airfield gets fogged in, the theory is that we switch on the radio beam, and then fly on in through the clag, using the 'blind' approach system. I've never used it for real, and I've never met any other pilot who has used it. Nevertheless, all squadron pilots coming along these days are required to hack through a week's intensive course on the beam, plus a written examination."

"In other words," Frank rounded things off, "it was all just a waste of time."

"Well now." I had to smile at that one, "it all depends on what you mean by a waste of time. Let me tell you about one side issue on that course, and then you tell me if it was a waste of time." I could sense the beginning of a resigned look spreading across the Flight Engineer's face. "Don't roll over," I encouraged. "It gets better. True, the beam course itself was a bit of a ho-hum affair but, as a few of us found out, it wasn't the only game in town. There was this well put together maiden, and she had the copyright on some cute little tricks of her own." That relit Frank's interest. "She was about five-foot-seven, had deep auburn hair, all topped off with the sort of figure that could start people talking to themselves."

"It all came to pass in the living quarters area; a single room for each pilot. I've an idea that these had been for 'officers only' at one time. The beam course had barged in on the place, creating a few loose ends here and there. Bubbles — I never did get her name — was one of the loose ends. As sergeants we didn't warrant room service, a detail which our newly acquired batwoman completely ignored. She continued caring for her residents with untiring enthusiasm, regardless of rank; applying the widest possible interpretation to her role. Her chiefs may have thought the functions of this WAAF were limited to making up beds, sweeping floors, and snaking along with early morning teas. She herself had different ideas."

"The lady had seen the mundanity of the set-up, and had quietly added a few amendments of her own; little extras that would be to the benefit of all." I could sense Frank's interest building. "While we were there, the weather was heating up nicely, a fact that had not gone unnoticed by our enterprising caretaker. She would wait until a room was occupied, preferably with the occupant slothing it out on his bed. A gentle knock would herald an equally gentle entrance. It was time to give the place the once over, she would announce. Would you mind? And so the show got on the road, the preliminary pitch being slipped in after the dusting routine had been underway for a few seconds."

" 'It's rather close in here,' the maiden would murmur quietly. 'Would there be any objections if I took off my jacket?' And so we lost the outer armour. A few minutes more and in came the main chance. 'It's still pretty warm in here,' would be the clincher from our busy little cleaner. 'Would you mind if I cooled off a bit more?'" Now our Flight Engineer was really paying attention. "That opened the flood gates, Frank. She yanked her regulation blouse out of her regulation skirt, and undid all the buttons down the front. This peeloff may well have helped the lady herself to cool down, but it did my temperature no good at all."

"There was only one way to dust the window, and that was to lean right across the muttonhead on the bed. The bra, together with its contents, was pointing straight at me, its double-trouble separated by a cleavage that looked like a replay of the Grand Canyon. The bare midriff, too, was just a nudge away. All that was left to accomplish by the nut on the bed was to reach out, toss a duster out of contention, and click two bra hooks into neutral. "You can see the major problem I faced here, Frank."

There was a pause to let the Engineer fully appreciate the problem.

"Push this generously contrived situation back into someone's face, and I could have ended up with Bubbles never coming around again to dust my room. It was a situation calling for measured compromise. After all, who needs a dusty room?"

Frank was leaning back in his seat now, smiling broadly at the approaching local scene.

"I take it all back." He had reappraised. "That beam course was well worth every mind-boggling second!"

As R-Roger swung majestically from downwind to crosswind leg in the circuit, ready for the slide down to the runway, I was aware of Harry standing behind me in the walkway beside his radio.

"You were quite right, Harry," I assured our Wireless Operator.

"Right about what, Skip?"

"It always does sound a whole lot easier in the briefing room. Once off the deck, and this caper quickly develops into a game of chance and chicanery. You just know that someone'll win, and someone'll lose. This time around, all that we lost in R-Roger was the aiming point."

The final turn lined Roger up with the runway.

"Stradishall control. 26. Finals."

"26. You're clear to land."

CHAPTER
TWO

Well, Hello There!

Timing, as all the great romantics assure us, is everything. Maybe so, but there is nothing like a generous dollop of luck to help things along.

The names on the Flight Room blackboard were restless, uneasy tenants. Some finished their tour of duty and moved on; others were axed out of the sky and never seen again. Skill and experience had nothing much to do with the outcome. There was but one arbiter.

Lady Luck called the shots. If she looked favourably on your destiny, you were flying free. If she frowned, you were down the tubes like yesterday's breakfast. That was the basic reality of operational flying.

For the moment, at least, timing and luck were flying right along with us. No sooner did I become accustomed to being a pilot officer than the chiefs elevated that to flying officer.

Still the names continued to fall out of the spaces on the blackboard. Flight Lieutenants Hanson, Broadman and Jones had survived their operational flying, and were now posted elsewhere, certainly carrying with them many horrific memories they would probably

134

never share with their grandchildren. One of the Brits, Flying Officer Maund, and two Australian pilots, each one complete with crew, had all been killed in action.

As spaces were created on the blackboard, the Flight Commander moved our names up to a more exalted space. I was moved up in rank to flight lieutenant. Only the ruthless, ever-changing, never-stand-still business of a wartime squadron could warrant such bewildering surges of promotion. Incredibly, I had moved from a non-commissioned flight sergeant to a flight lieutenant in exactly seven weeks. The only trick to achieve this was simply to stay alive! As I moved up, I had to make the confusing leap from Sergeants' Mess to Officers' Mess.

Squadron Leader Bass did everything he could to make the switchover a smooth one, aware of the trauma involved. He moved my gear in his car from crew barrack block to my room in the Mess, introducing me to the dining-room steward as we passed through the building. Later, the boss made sure the Sergeant in charge of the bar knew I was one of his "B" Flight organisation. This unwrinkling of the highway into the Officers' Mess was most helpful.

Two nights after my arrival, and still just a sprog pilot officer, I was trying to disappear behind a whisky and soda in one of the darker corners of the bar. That was when I saw her face and top half at the other end of the counter. It was Flying Officer Melville, the lady who had been dealing out the intelligence information at our first and second attacks on Wesel. She was laughing at something Flight Lieutenant Ian Cameron had just said. The remark was well worth the effort,

135

whatever it had been. Unsmiling, this intelligence officer looked great; laughing, she could start a revolution. Trouble was, how could I get close enough to meet a maiden like this, even if I could think up something funny to say? Two weeks later, I was helped along by a dash of fortuity. Even here on the deck, Lady Luck was holding my hand.

With no day or night operation lined up for our lot on this particular morning, the boss filled in as best he could. The two gunners and I were pointed up into the air for fighter evasion practice, while the other four members of the crew were directed to the firing ranges. Our exercise in the air began to unwind right from the start.

First, all the plugs on one of our port engines had to be changed. Then the rendezvous point with the fighter got fuzzed around. By the time the camera guns had run out of film on the corkscrewing exercises, the three of us were well and truly late for lunch. The boss had to pacify catering facilities, arranging for late lunches for Ivor and Clin at the Sergeants' Mess, and for me at the Officers' Mess.

By 1430 hours I had the dining-room to myself, the staff already busy setting the tables for dinner. Nearest to the servery a table had been arranged for the late lunchers, two places all tooled up and waiting. Obviously some other "doughnut" had also slipped out of phase with the proper lunch time.

"So what was your excuse?" asked the voice coming at me from behind my head somewhere. I was sitting with my back to the entrance, and had to do a half-swing around so I could fit a body to the voice. Now there was a surprise to set the pulses racing: Flying Officer Melville no less. I started to get up.

"For heaven's sake, stay down, but don't lose sight of my question. I'll bet you have a better excuse than I do."

The manner was friendly and relaxed, the smile backed up by an easy, flowing confidence.

"Not much of a reason, really," I had to admit. "First, a Lancaster went sick on me, and then a Spitfire pilot and I lost each other in the clouds. By the time we quit playing hide and seek, well . . . here I am. Late."

The WAAF officer smiled.

"Just as I thought," she said. "Your excuse is much more believable than mine. I was . . .", she looked around furtively to make sure none of the dining-room staff was within hearing range, resuming in a more muted tone, ". . . over at Group HQ picking up some papers. Yes, I could easily have taken lunch over there, but I never feel at ease in that place. The dining-room is knee-deep in high ranking brass. Every time I ask someone to pass the salt, I have this crazy idea that I should get up and salute." We both laughed at that one. "By the way," she enlightened, "my name is Judy Melville."

"I'm Philip Gray," I volunteered.

"Now there's a solid Chinese name," Judy quipped. "Which part of Scotland are you from?"

Allowing the question to hang there for a bit, I met the lady's expectant glance across the table. All smiles and explanation, I gave her the answer.

"Since joining this war I've answered that question many times. The come-back has nearly always been the same. 'Where the hell is that?' But . . . for old times' sake, here we go again. I was born in a little township called Ladybank, right in the middle of Fife, but I've lived mostly in Broughty Ferry, on the fringes of Dundee. You've never heard of either one. Right?"

I could tell by the satisfied, cheeky grin that there could be a new answer this time.

"Wrong. I am indeed aware of both of them," she said triumphantly. "I was stationed at Leuchars Aerodrome for six months before transferring to Bomber Command a year ago. How about that?"

I was staggered. Not only had I finally found someone who had heard of my home turf, but someone who had actually been resident there.

"That's truly amazing," I had to admit. "You'll have to let me buy you a drink on the strength of that one."

"You're on," Judy agreed, "but right now we had better get out of here. I think we have overstayed our welcome. Anyway, some of us have work to do."

She shot off to the Intelligence Section with her papers. I used the stairs to reach my first floor room. If I ever met that Spitfire pilot who had helped push back the morning schedule, I certainly owed him a drink, too. Without his help I would never have found myself in a one-on-one situation with Judy Melville.

Cheers!

CHAPTER
THREE

Don't Creep Back

"It's a ruthless business now, isn't it?"

I turned toward Harry to try to make some sense of his outburst. All three of us were walking down through the Administration blocks toward the Flight Offices, at least Jack and I convinced that the conversation was about the film we had all seen the night before. This had been a comedy.

"You sure we all saw the same film?" I queried, directing the question at Harry. But it was obvious from the clouded, sombre expression on the Wireless Operator's face that he had been merely walking along the edge of our film review, his real thoughts somewhere else altogether. He ignored my question.

"They've changed the rules of war in the air these days," Harry continued in the same aggrieved tone. "Whatever happened to the ethics of World War One?"

"Come on, my friend, you've been reading too many stories in the *Boys' Own Paper*," suggested Jack.

"That's not what I'm talking about," Harry countered, "and you know it. Just think what happens these days if we get hit and have to jump for our lives. If you pull the ripcord too soon, and the opposition still has some bullets in the rack, he's liable to blow you away as you hang there helplessly on the ends of parachute strings."

We walked on in silence for a bit digesting this undoubted fact of life, the trivial talk about last night's film having fallen flat on its face. As schoolboys, we had all heard tales of that earlier conflict, seen the films, read the accounts. Harry was right. In the air, at least, World War One had been a much more honourable affair than this rumble in which we were now engaged.

There had been those epics of dawn patrols, scarves streaming in the wind, gallantry acknowledged with a wave of the hand. Even the battles were fought out to a code of ethics. When a brave combatant was killed in action, on whichever side, the lone, unarmed enemy fighter plane would make the pilgrimage back across the front lines. It was perfectly visible; it flew low; it was expected. There would then be the dip of the aircraft's nose as a farewell salute over the grave, and a wreath dropped to the ground to acknowledge the loss of a worthy opponent.

This was the era of Baron Manfred von Richthofen, the Red Baron, one of Germany's most feared and respected fighter aces. Downing eighty Allied planes during his spectacular career, this flyer led his fighter squadron with chivalry and panache. Von Richthofen must have dropped many wreaths from the cockpit of his bright red plane before he, too, was cut down, his star falling during the last month of that historical set-to.

Jack tried to bring us down to earth again.

"With all good intentions, Harry," he suggested, "this war, too, may well have started with threads of chivalry trying their very best to survive the onslaught, but the pattern quickly changed. Such ruthless debacles as the bombing of Warsaw, Rotterdam and Liverpool brushed such things as ethics into the dustbin. Why, our own city of London has been bombed quite indiscriminately."

Harry nodded in agreement, but the distant look in his eyes had him at another place in another time. Maybe he was still riding down out of the sun, white scarf streaming behind, guns chattering from the cockpit of his World War One fighter. I felt some sympathy for our wireless operator. Could be that the lad had arrived here just a war too late.

"Ethics may be the one to bug you, Harry," I said, "but that bloody photograph is the one that screws my guts into knots."

"What photograph?" queried the puzzled radio man.

Jack was well aware of the camera work to which I referred.

"Phil's talking about the picture we are forced to take every time we cross a target."

"Oh, that one," said Harry, "but that's always been part of the act, hasn't it?"

"No, not really," answered Jack. "Let's say we owe that one to human nature."

The Air Bomber didn't enlarge on his statement, and Harry didn't insist, but I knew what he meant.

The early months of World War Two had begun in mellow-tone, dubbed The Phoney War. The Germans started with high-flying reconnaissance aircraft on regular runs over Britain, while we retaliated by dropping plane loads of propaganda leaflets over their cities.

The phase soon passed, bombs replacing leaflets. The Royal Air Force set forth on one of the longest, costliest, most destructive, and finally, most murderously efficient bombing campaigns the world had ever witnessed. The chancy beginning was so different from the thousand-bomber armadas that rode forth in later years.

At the start, it was all uphill for Bomber Command. Those gallant, early-war pilots in their Hampden, Blenheim, and Whitley bombers were asked to fight a battle against almost impossible odds, their deeds chronicled in awe, their names spoken in reverence by their peers. No radar assisted in those first months; the bomb loads were puny; the opposition, both on the ground and in the air, was formidable; and weather played a large part in the success or failure of a mission.

"Bombers' Moon" — lovely moonlit countryside and clear skies — was ideal bombing conditions for obvious reasons. A year or so later, as radar began to filter in, the expression became meaningless.

The crews of those brave little tadpole-shaped Hampdens and accident-prone Whitleys never faltered, buying valuable time for their country while bigger and better bombers were planned and built. Grim weather conditions, night fighters, collisions, flak, someone else's bombs, searchlights, faulty engines, bombs fused but refusing to go — truly, the hazards were endless. On one occasion meteorological forecasts proved to be disastrously in error. Seventy bombers failed to return to their bases. The luxury of radar, with the all-seeing eye of H2S and the accuracy of Gee-H, would have brushed this problem aside.

As the system was to find out, though, even heroes have a breakdown point. Honour and moral fibre are variables. Like pain, the threshold is different in each one of us. To submit an aircrew to the savage impact and shock of an enemy target just once was one thing, to continue such demands every few days was something else. The scars began to show.

In people, imperceptibly at first but with accelerating clarity, it could be the hands or figures forever shaking, head jerking at odd times, the use of liquor or wakey-wakey tablets to lean on, endless and meaningless chatter, right down to complete nervous disintegration. Such things could be temporary, or they could scar the more vulnerable for a lifetime. Once freed from Royal Air Force flying, some pilots never left the ground again.

The second half of the legacy, the targets, was another matter altogether. In this area, our reconnaissance aircraft brought back photographs which raised eyebrows. As the assessors at Bomber Command swung their powerful magnifying equipment across the print-outs, the problems could not be ignored. More and more, bombs were falling short of the target, the shortfall getting progressively worse as the campaign continued. If allowed to go on, this situation would ensure immunity to the coking plants and munition factories, while the cows and milkmaids in the fields would find themselves in the front line.

The phenomenon these assessors were monitoring was the infamous "creepback", one more foible of human nature. Our leaders knew only too well how cruelly the odds were stacked against their flyers.

The Luftwaffe, in the opening war years, was superior in every area of operations. If the anti-aircraft fire and searchlight cover for most major cities in the Third Reich were considered legendary, then those throughout the Ruhr Valley were awesome. Cities such as Dusseldorf, Essen, Dortmund, Wuppertal and Cologne could cover their valuables with an almost impenetrable umbrella of steel, so thick, reckoned the pilots of earlier years, that you could get out and walk on it. Try to front up to this well-groomed terror night after night, and creepback wasn't just a possibility, it was inevitable.

Some of those early heroes, providing they could go on surviving, and providing they had the choice, would reach the point where even bravery baulked at the endless carnage. So, down went their bombs just that little bit short of the inferno, a quick about-turn for home, and they could melt away into the anonymity of the night. The solution for this problem was to make sure that no one was given the luxury of choice. That brought the camera to centre stage.

Every bomber now had a camera set into a housing on the underside of the fuselage. As the air bomber pressed the plunger stud to send our cargo of retribution across the target area, so, too, did he trigger the time mechanism of the camera. Approximately twenty-five seconds later the shutter clicked and hopefully recorded a photograph of the target. The negative became a passport of credibility for the crew, proof that they had been right over the target at the time of the exposure. The days of stopping short and "this-is-close-enough" were over.

Come back now with a blank negative, caused, say, by a sudden steep turn to avoid another bomber, or by initiating corkscrew action in the presence of enemy fighters, and the Flight Commander would demur and possibly go along with the explanation. Come back with a blank negative a second time, and the explanation would be made to the Squadron Commander; each back scrutinised closely for any sign of yellow streaks. It might be preferable to be shot down rather than return a third time with a blank negative. The eagle eye of the camera had banished creepback.

I smiled when I thought of Harry and his preoccupation with the chivalry of the dawn patrols of yesteryear. Riding through the hell of today up to the point of "bombs away" was enough for most of us to take. Then being required to hold fast for another thirty seconds — flying straight and level to ensure a good photograph — was nerve-twisting stuff. True, we had carried out only half a dozen operational flights so far, but the tension of those hairy thirty seconds was to stay with me.

For the survivors, it was a time-span that could turn young boys into old men, the slow measured count scarring its path across their sanity. For the losers, grinding through another half minute of foreverness was to be their last conscious act, either cannon shells or flak blowing their dreams and fears into the hinterlands of eternity.

CHAPTER
FOUR

Battle Order

Following the far-away explosion, I seemed to be floating upside down, feet in the air, like a piece of driftwood on the tide line. The banging came again, as did consciousness and reality. Someone was knocking persistently on the bedroom door.

"Yes," was the only response I could muster.

"0430, Sir," a voice told me. "Your early call."

"Oh yes . . . thank you."

"Now, you're sure you're awake, Sir?"

"I'm sure . . ."

Jack and I shared the same room, and the rumblings from his bed space suggested that the call had also ruined his sleep.

"This is ridiculous," complained the Air Bomber. "Why can't we bomb these places at a more civilised time? I'm sure the Germans would be quite agreeable."

"The only consolation," I suggested, struggling up to a sitting position, "is that the poor sods defending whatever we are about to hit will also have had an early call. They never know when we're liable to turn up."

★ ★ ★

Another beautiful night's sleep was being ruined in the village of Buer, just outside the city of Gelsenkirchen at the north-east corner of the Ruhr Valley. Helga Klonstadt had been hustled into the cold awareness of her bedroom, the hands on her noisy little alarm clock pointing at 0430 hours. "Why, oh why," she thought, "can't this long, senseless war just go away?"

The Wehrmacht Sergeant was well aware that she was part of an elite group, the anti-aircraft shield protecting the Ruhr Basin. This area was reputed to have more guns to the square mile than any other place on earth. Allied flyers knew very well that Helga and her colleagues were true professionals, their work fine-honed by years of practice.

The chatter and banter across the Briefing Room at Stradishall muted and died, all eyes following the Wing Commander of 186 Squadron as he crossed the platform to the blackboard. Always there was a curtain drawn across the face of the board, one of several security measures taken to lessen the chances of our intent filtering prematurely into enemy hands. The door of the room was locked. Service police were stationed all around the complex. Our before-Ops meal of eggs, bacon and toast was served in a dining-room right next to the Briefing Room, the two sharing a connecting door.

Every public telephone within a wide area around bomber stations "died" when their squadrons were about to launch an attack, coming back into service when the planes were well on their way to the target. What we were attending was the general briefing.

The first briefing, the nuts and bolts preparation by the navigators, had started one hour before, giving them information about weather conditions as well as technical details of tracks to be followed by the whole bomber stream. From all of this, the navigators would work out and plot the courses to be flown, estimating times of arrival at the various turning points.

Navigators knew most of the secrets long before the rest of us were allowed into the Briefing Room. To rectify this deficiency, the WingCo pulled the curtain clear of the blackboard.

"The Ruhr again, gentlemen," he confirmed, "Gelsenkirchen to be precise. You have good back-up this time. I'm coming with you."

Wing Commander Giles gave the general picture of heights and courses there and back, the strength of the attack, the name of the synthetic oil installation we were aiming to eradicate. The Intelligence Officer told us about possible fighter opposition, and the latest position of the bomb line. This was a line which snaked down through the maps and charts as a parallel to the front line, but was always ten miles inside enemy territory. We were not allowed to bomb, or the fighters to strafe, within this sensitive area between the front and bomb lines.

The Bombing Leader gave the names of the Gee-H leaders, and the two Lancasters which would fly with them to form V or Vic formations. The lead plane would use specialised radar equipment to pinpoint the precise spot to be bombed.

In the final act, of course, Gee-H or not, it was the air bomber of each Lancaster who was responsible for dropping the bombs. Jack brought the fuses of these 500-pounders alive and more or less controlled the bomber on the final run-up to the target. He was also responsible for ensuring that none of the bombs was left hanging stubbornly in the bomb bay.

The engineers were told what the petrol load would be and which cross-feed levers to use. The wireless operators were briefed on which channels to monitor on the run to the target, exactly when they could safely start sending out information on the way back, and given details about the various emergency frequencies.

Then came the Meteorological Officer with the weather details, information vital for the success of the attack and our own survival.

The Flight Commanders, "A" and "B" Flights, rounded off the briefing with a word for the pilots — "bus drivers" as we were known. We were to fly as tight a formation group as possible. If separated from our Gee-H leader for any reason, we were to try to attach to another leader. If this proved impractical, then we should bomb on our own Gee-H coordinates. If cut out by flak, we were to estimate the damage and work out the destiny of the crew and the plane from the assessment. It would obviously be preferable to land on the Allied side of the bomb line. Certain structural damage could call for a compromise solution.

There would be times when the bomber was perfectly airworthy, until the pilot tried to put it on the ground. On these occasions it would be safest to use one of the two specially equipped emergency airfields on the south coast of England. These landing fields were endowed with long, long runways with an abundance of fire wagons and ambulances, plus huge bulldozers.

I was always fascinated by the last visual we had as we left the Briefing Room. This was a huge, coloured portrait of the leader of Bomber Command, Air Chief Marshal Sir Arthur Harris, hanging above the exit. A telling message printed in bold lettering underneath assured us: "When he says you go, YOU GO!"

The German Army transport swept the north side of Gelsenkirchen, picking up Helga Klonstadt and at least twenty other gun controllers as it rumbled on. The destination was the site of Anti-Aircraft Force No 32, whose primary function was to protect the Gelsenberg Benzine Plant at Nordstern, but whose guns also shared in the general defence of that segment of the city.

Helga was in command of Unit 15. This consisted of four heavy anti-aircraft guns, their firing and alignment controlled by the Sergeant. The Gun Controller achieved this supervision with the help of radar equipment, its signals beaming skyward to probe for and identify enemy intruders. True, visual daytime contact was the ideal, but firing by night or through thick cloud cover was no problem.

★　★　★

R-Roger was climbing smoothly up to our bombing height, the Lancaster now on its third of four courses. The bomber stream never approached a target head on, but invariably did a round-the-houses approach to confuse the enemy. Clusters of Luftwaffe fighters would be scrambled and sent to combat height over selected cities, hoping to pick off several of the lumbering, less manoeuvrable bombers when they eventually arrived at the target. As always, Lady Luck called the shots. Sometimes these fighter controllers got it wrong; many times they hit a bulls'-eye.

"About fifty miles to go, Phil," Gerry informed. "There will be a new course to steer in about three minutes."

Roger was now flying level at its run-in height of 18,000 feet.

"Deal's the same as before, everybody," I reiterated one more time. "Those who can, keep rubber necking all around the sky. We don't want one of these crafty bastards creeping up our ass when we least expect it."

"OK, Skip." "Understood, Skip." "Right, Phil," came acknowledgements from the two gunners in their turrets, and Jack in the nose of the aircraft. Frank was on his feet, leaning against the right side of the aircraft. He said nothing, but gave me the thumbs up. The Wireless Operator and Navigator were tucked away in their little offices behind me, and could not check for enemy fighters.

"New course 170 degrees, Phil," Gerry ordered.

"170 degrees," I repeated as I started the turn. We were well back in the stream of three hundred and forty

Lancasters, so the spearhead bombers must already be causing concern in the north-east corner of the Ruhr.

All anti-aircraft units in the Ruhr Valley were standing to, their first salvo of shells in position, their long sleek gun barrels flexing around expectantly toward the north. Word of our approach was running ahead of us. Helga Klonstadt had switched on her radar long ago, and was already intently studying its empty but rather beautifully shaded green surface. The safety cap was off the firing button. The Controller was estimating the bomber stream approach line and setting up the initial line of aim.

Gone now were the dreams of sleepy mornings and sunny days. This was war. This was her homeland. Win or lose, the Controller of Unit 15 would endeavour to cause the maximum amount of pain and grief for the approaching bomber stream.

"Flak up front."

Our Lancaster was still well out from the target, but my warning was to alert everyone that crunch time was here.

"And just in case you wondered," I slipped in, "it looks as accurate and heavy as ever."

"I'd like to screw these blonde-headed gun controllers into the ground," grumbled Clin from the rear turret.

"You never know," I volunteered. "They could be very good to their mothers."

"Screw them, too," Clin came back.

"Before you do, keep your eyes peeled back there, Clin. We don't want any unwelcome bullets up our bum."

"Wilco."

As our operational career had developed, we all realised that the two tactical attacks on Wesel were really soft touches. Being beginners at the time, we had thought these set-to's were tough, dangerous assignments. Oh, they were hazardous affairs up to a point, 186 Squadron losing one or two aircraft and crews during their execution, but the big boomers were the established city or industrial clashes. The protectors of such places were ready for us; they really knew the score.

Today, from the moment our attack got underway, medium and heavy ack-ack artillery units pumped up shells just as fast as they could reload and re-focus. Sooner or later these gunners would get lucky.

Even two miles short of the target we could see the latest shells exploding all across the action and, equally intimidating, all the spluttering smoke puffs of their predecessors hanging there in their hundreds like delegates of doom and disaster. Common sense should have registered that these plumes of spent flak were harmless obscenities left behind by a piece of the war we had just missed. In reality, they looked terrifying, smearing their unwanted presence across a beautiful blue sky, seeming to fill our whole world as we slid into the target area.

Experience was no friend. All aspects of our operational flying, even the violent bits, were happening in a pattern. It was uncanny. As we hardened to the dangers, all of the agony in these later raids would register in detail.

"This friggin' flak is about as heavy as I've seen it," Frank murmured in a low tone, staring poker-faced through the front glass work, talking more to himself than to anyone in particular.

"And it's bloody accurate," I added.

"Maybe they're trying t . . ." was as far as Frankie got.

The Mid-upper Gunner cut in on the intercom.

"Kite going down on our port side, Skip, about 5,000 feet below us." "It's a Lanc, and the tail unit's been blown clean off."

"Keep your eye open for parachutes, Blondie," I told him, fighting to be heard above the clamour going on all around us, "but watch your own back too."

I took a brief glance through the side window and saw the broken bomber start its slow spiral, the tail unit, with the Rear Gunner's turret still intact, falling away rapidly. I could only hope that the poor gunner had managed to back-somersault clear, dreading the stronger suspicion that he was still in there and wounded. But that's about all the time and attention I could spare. There were things taking place outside my own front windscreen I wished I didn't have to watch.

"Five 'chutes came out of that Lanc, Skip." This information came from the Engineer.

"The other two poor sods must have bought it," reasoned the Rear Gunner.

Noise and organised chaos were all around us now as we started the bomb run: the flashes, the smells, the explosions, the turbulence, the cannon stutter, and the unexpected, all doing their very best to numb us into a state of immobility and stupefaction.

Mixed with the internal radio chatter and the external exploding ack-ack shells, a spoof detonated with one helluva bang quite close by. This was a scare device which the ground defences mixed in with their regular shells. It was apparently a thinly encased projectile filled mostly with gunpowder and miscellaneous bits of wire, fabric, and other such factory rubbish. The spectacular explosion was relatively harmless, but it did appear remarkably like one of our own bombers blowing up, which was exactly the effect it was meant to convey. The hope was that it would panic the more inexperienced operators in the bomber stream, their alarm causing them to collide with another bomber close by.

The Air Bomber and the Navigator now controlled the plane between them. Just as they were about to get into their set patter, Clin broke through the build-up from his rear turret.

"Christ, Skip, that friggin' plane behind us has drifted forward. It's almost above us now, and it's got its bomb doors wide open."

Blondie must have looked up above his head.

"If he presses the tit now, we're friggin' history," threw in a very agitated Mid-upper.

I flicked the wheel over to port, and pushed in heavily on the left rudder, losing my Gee-H leader as I did so. This business was delicate enough without playing peek-a-boo with someone else's hardware.

"Jack! Gerry!" I knew the time was slipping away. "You're on your own now. I've had to ditch our Gee-H leader because of that gumball up there."

Hooked up to the internal RT, both of them were perfectly aware of the situation.

"Right, Phil," Gerry came back, icy calm. "Steer 273 degrees and maintain height. We've got about ninety seconds."

"Bomb doors open," ordered Jack.

No one ever mentioned it, but the same thought must have been churning the stomachs of every member of Bomber Command as they passed through this vulnerable part of the attack. There we all were, hanging above the target at anything from 18,000 to 21,000 feet, bomb doors wide open, and our 12,000 pounds of TNT exposed and swinging in the breeze. All it would take to past tense us would be a hit by a red hot slice of maverick shrapnel and . . .

Gerry watched as the two tiny triangles on the Gee-II radar screen got ready to hold hands.

Jack lined up the plane.

"Shade left, Phil." "Bit more." "Back right a little." "Steady." "Steady."

The blips on the Gee-H radar screen clicked together.

"Hit the button, Jack."

"Bombs away!"

The Lancaster reared up in relief as our contribution to Gelsenkirchen's ill health got on its way. This final

157

phase of the bomb run had consumed a lifetime of thirty seconds, and now the second half-minute, another lifetime, started to unreel.

The camera's delayed-action switch had engaged in unison with the bomb release button, and now we had to fly very straight and very level to record that all-important photograph. At this delicate moment, one of the ack-ack shells came in really close. The explosion seemed to punch up the rear of the plane, its effect echoing through the control column and rudder pedals.

"Christ, that was close," said an ashen-faced Frank.

I didn't have time to answer.

"I've been hit," someone yelled over the RT, the voice sounding both shocked and surprised.

"That you, Clin?" I asked, trying to pin things down.

"Not me, Skip," assured the Rear Gunner.

"It's me — Blondie."

"Who's free to help?"

"I'm free," said Gerry. "I'm on my way back."

"Where did it get you, Ivor?" I asked. "Just how bad is it?"

I was still trying to hold the Lancaster straight and level for that photograph, hoping like hell that someone else wouldn't have a go at us.

"I've been hit on the face somewhere," the Mid-upper answered.

I looked along at Frank.

"What d'you know about firing 303s, Frank?"

"Not hellish much, but if you're asking, I'll have a go."

158

"Fair enough," I acknowledged, and Frank, too, headed back toward the centre of the plane, leaving me alone in the cabin. Since sending our bombs on their way, Jack was now on his feet and manning the guns in the front turret.

Now it was Harry's turn.

"That friggin' flak has sliced off all my outside aerials. I can't get a thing on the radio."

"Then maybe you can give Gerry a hand fixing up Blondie."

"OK."

Harry eventually plugged his helmet into a spare RT socket halfway down the Lancaster's interior.

"Blondie has been hit with splinters I think, Skip," he told me, "but it's not too drastic."

"Thank goodness for that. How's the turret itself?" I asked. "Is it usable?"

"It looks more usable than my radio set," Harry lamented with an injured edge to his voice.

I had just seen another Lancaster badly hit by flak over on our starboard side, but this didn't seem to be the time to depress anyone with information like that. The big bomber was literally falling to pieces as I watched.

"You in the mid-upper turret, Frank?"

"Yip, I'm here, Skip, but I'm not quite sure what to do. Anyway, I think Blondie will manage to come back up here in a little while."

"Those who can," I ran it past them one more time, "keep your eyes wide open. The far side of the target is one of the favourite places for these bloody FWs to jump us."

Mercifully, the German fighters left us alone, and we were only too happy to leave Gelsenkirchen.

"I'm back in the turret, Skip."

"Sure you're OK?" I asked.

"I'm fine."

"Good on you."

Back at base, we were able to see for ourselves the punishment poor old R-Roger had taken from that ack-ack shell. All the back section of our friend was full of holes, radio aerials trailing along the concrete like abandoned fishing lines. To build up the drama, the Padre and the Station Group Captain gave us special attention as we disgorged from the motor transport. I'm sure Blondie was happy to tell them the story, explaining why half of his face was covered with a shell dressing. The rest of us were happy that his cuts were just hit and run affairs, and would soon go away. Apparently a piece of shrapnel had cut into one side of the turret bubble and exited through the opposite side, ricocheting a shard of splintered plexiglass from the turret wall across our Mid-upper's face as it did so.

The first hint of bad news always began to show in the locker room. This time, as the minutes plundered their path into the future, fourteen lockers remained untouched, mute guardians now holding their contents in trust for posterity. The original owners would never return. 186 Squadron had lost two crews and two Lancasters to the flak and cannon shells over Gelsenkirchen.

When we calculated the various positions in the bomber stream, that must have been Flight Lieutenant Cameron's Lancaster I saw going down as the boys were busy fixing Blondie's wounds. F/Lt Cameron was an Australian, the one I had seen making Judy Melville laugh that evening in the bar. It was so sad.

Equally sad was the fate of Jimmy Randell and his crew. Hit over the target by flak, Jimmy had nursed his Lancaster all the way home to within three fields of Stradishall. There, so tantalisingly close to sanctuary, the plane had given up the fight and spread itself and its crew all over the grass. There were no survivors.

Helga Klonstadt switched off the radar equipment and snapped the safety cap over the firing button. It had been quite a successful day. The preliminary count reckoned that fifteen bombers had been clawed down from the stream, most by anti-aircraft fire. That was fifteen machines and crews that couldn't come back tomorrow. On the down side, the Nordstern Oil Refinery was wrecked almost beyond repair.

CHAPTER
FIVE

Their Names Were Never Mentioned

Grief was always a problem. By the time we had returned from one skirmish, the plans for the next were already coming in on the wires. Other crews would man the guns and push the throttles forward but, as sure as the Lord made small potatoes, the battle would go on. So, too, would more crews get the chop, creating more anguish, more grief.

As one line of names after another had to be erased from our Flight Room blackboard, their owners hammered out of contention, we, the survivors, found ourselves overpowered by the pace of the distress. To cope with this relentless emotional strain, members of aircrew were forced to create a ritual of their own. It had to be fast. It had to be effective. They had to be careful that the sheer weight of woe did not overwhelm.

To the casual observer, these grieving rites could have been seen as macabre and insensitive. Most people might take a lifetime to grieve the loss of, say, six to ten close friends. In this iffy pastime of spreading desolation over the German landscape, we could lose dozens of known faces in a single day, several of them being personal friends. How can normality meet such a challenge? How can ordinary human emotions cope with loss on this scale? There had to be cauterisation or it could have led to insanity. Unlike I Pagliacci, we couldn't go about our business with tears in our eyes . . .

"Drinks all round, barman," ordered the WingCo. "I'll sign the tab."

The night was young. We had a long way to go. Debriefing had come and gone. The trauma of the locker room had been brazened out. Shower, shave, shampoo — even dinner — had all passed in semi-silence.

Squadron Leader Bass set up the drinks again. Then Squadron Leader Jason, then Flight Lieutenant Hardy, then . . . and so it went on.

That specific evening, images of Flight Lieutenant Cameron and Flight Lieutenant Randell, and any or all of their bomber crews, may have flitted in and out of our thoughts but their names were never mentioned. By the time we walked through the Flight Room door tomorrow, any reference to their physical presence would have faded from the blackboard as though they had never been. In truth, their sacrifice would ride on down the highway of glory for all eternity.

The barman set up the drinks once more, this time for me. Earlier on in the evening several WAAF officers had been present in the bar as usual, but they knew exactly where this night was headed, and had melted away some time ago. This night's operational Lancasters had long since flown off into the gloom. A crescendo of laughter and eerie merriment began to build up around the bar. Fairly soon now there would be no more pain.

Someone, I think it was Wing Commander Giles, jumped onto one of the tables, threw off his jacket, and called for another drink. That drink and still other glasses appeared from the smoky shadows as if by magic.

"Off, off, off," someone shouted, and everyone else seemed to take up the chant on cue. One by one the WingCo flung off his shoes, socks, trousers, shirt, singlet, until he stood there in nothing but his underpants. Drink in either hand, balancing precariously on the table top, the Squadron boss now had his hands outstretched, making zooming noises and diving motions with his arms. The racket was full pitch, and the flak started to fly around the room. Those of us spread here and there in different parts of the bar bunched newspaper pages into balls, set fire to them, and heaved them at the WingCo. He, in turn, tried to parry and avoid the missiles, still holding the drinks at arm's length.

Someone got up on another table, then someone else. Soon we were all over the target again, planes rolling through, flak flying in all directions, only this time there were no losers. No one got shot down. Even at this stage though, anaesthetised by Gilbey's Gin and Johnnie Walker, some sixth sense told us that we had to hurry.

Another operational flight was underway right now, our crews slicing through the flak, searchlights and night fighters. Tomorrow there might be other names dropping off the blackboard, other faces to be exorcised, and the charade to cut the edge off the sadness would start rolling all over again. There was only one part of the story, the Killing Game if you prefer the other title, that was forever misting off into the land of "we'll-talk-about-that-tomorrow". This was the question no one ever dared to ask, even of himself. Next time, would we be tanking up yet again to forget someone else, or would all the someone elses be tanking up to forget me?

Judy Melville poked her head around the bar door earlier on in the piece, long before the WingCo had eased into his striptease act and the flak had started to scythe about the room. The Intelligence Officer was obviously looking for someone specific. We both knew I still owed her the drink I had promised, but this would not have been a good time to honour the obligation. Other faces and other memories were haunting us.

"Flight Lieutenant Philip Gray, if I'm not mistaken."

The assertive statement came from behind me. I had been walking back from the camp cinema. We had just been shown how Gary Cooper, as Sergeant York, had almost single-handedly won World War One — in monosyllables of course. The strains of the cinema's signature tune, *Strictly Instrumental*, were following me home, no doubt covering the sound of the footsteps that had been padding along behind me, barely audible on the grass. I stopped to turn and establish contact.

165

"Well, well," I was agreeably surprised, "if it isn't the pride of the intelligence network, Flying Officer Judy Melville."

Judy smiled at this extravagant declaration, but otherwise ignored it, slotting in a question of her own.

"Did all your boys get back from last night's affair?"

This was a reference to the night operation following our day attack on Gelsenkirchen. Ten of our lot had joined yet another attack on a different part of this same city. Fortunately, this time the Squadron had suffered no casualties, but only one of our planes had been able to return to base. Because of the rapidly deteriorating weather conditions, all of the remaining Lancasters had been diverted to other airfields, Flight Lieutenant Groves actually landing in France. Throughout the day they had all filtered back to Stradishall.

"They're all back now, I believe," I replied, "Lance Groves coming in just before dusk. Can I buy you that drink now?"

"Great idea," Judy beamed, starting to unbutton her greatcoat as we pushed through the front door of the Mess.

"I'll shoot up to my room with this coat. See you in the bar in two minutes."

"What's it to be?" I called after the retreating figure.

"Gin and anything."

"Right!"

No woman ever returned from anywhere in two minutes, of course, so I had time to ponder the niggling queries. Just how well had Judy known Ian Cameron? How long had she known him? How deep had their relationship been? Should I even mention the fact that he had got the chop? If the lady had lost something profound, I could hardly sit here and start in with frivolous small talk. After all, I had seen them just the once sharing a joke in the bar, my point of vantage being way across the other side of the room. Maybe it would be better if I just let things simmer along, allowing the lady to make the running. As Judy came in the door, I could see that this was one WAAF officer who did more for the uniform than the uniform did for her. We found a table.

"Here's to us."

"Cheers."

With common knowledge of such places as Dundee, Leuchars, and St. Andrews, we chattered on about these for a bit. An observation from Judy about our Ruhr attack came booming in out of the blue.

"That day attack on Gelsenkirchen yesterday appeared to have problems."

"Well," I started in cautiously, "186 was near the back of the stream. That's always a shaky place to be, especially over a target in 'Happy Valley'. The local gun club had no doubt got their eye well in by the time we arrived on the scene."

"We lost two Lancs," she said bluntly.

"We did indeed, but then I'd imagine we've lost more on earlier raids."

There was no escape now. Judy caught my eye square on across the table.

"I knew Flight Lieutenant Cameron quite well, you know."

Lady, I thought, you're pinning me down to the floor. What do I say now? And how well is "quite well"? A couple of movies? A roll in the hay? Or the complete now and for ever bit?

"He was a nice guy," I said, stating the obvious. "I walked down to the Flight Office with him once, and spoke with him a couple of times in the dining-room. I believe I saw you talking with him in the bar."

Judy insisted on lining up the drinks the second time around. I had watched her nod and smile to several people as she moved from the table to the bar, obviously well known to all of them. And that's the bit that puzzled me. This lady clearly wanted to talk about the pilot of this plane I had seen blown out of the sky, but then, she could have done that earlier with any one of these people. Most of them had been at 186 Squadron longer than I, so Judy would be closer to them.

The lady was about half way back to the table with the gin and whisky when the penny dropped. I was the one who had reported having seen the actual hit, and Judy, of course, as one of the intelligence officers, had access to all of the debriefing reports.

"Plenty of water you said." She smiled as she slid the glass across the table. "Hope the barman hasn't drowned it."

"That's fine," I assured her, not even bothering to look at the drink. On the way in we had both checked the Battle Order for tomorrow. The boys and I were on the programme. Time, I thought, to meet this thing head on.

"Judy," I said, as matter-of-factly as I dared, "I have a fair idea, from what I could gather around the debriefing room, that several people may have seen Ian's Lancaster go down, but that I was possibly the only one to see the actual hit. Am I right?"

The WAAF officer's eyes dropped to avert mine, the surface of the table now being studied with great interest. The intent stayed there for a little while. When Judy looked up again, the perky vivacious Intelligence Officer seemed to have melted into the table top, and I was confronted with a lady — a girl now — whose gentle, almost aching, expression was scrambling for a straw. The drinks were being ignored.

"You're right about the hit," she admitted without further explanation, her voice almost down to a whisper.

If ever there was a time when someone — anyone — should have been over there to hold on tightly to this girl, this was the time. It certainly couldn't be me, and certainly not in the middle of the Officers' Mess bar. Now it was my turn to look Judy in the eye.

"Before I utter another careless word, Judy, you'll have to bring the story in a whole lot closer. Just how well did you know this quiet Australian?"

She nodded in resignation and understanding.

"You surely deserve an answer to that one, and I'm sorry that you've been put in the gun like this, Philip."

After another small pause and a sip at her drink. Judy continued.

"The story, as you put it, goes back two years. In that time, once at Leuchars and once right here at

169

Stradishall, I have made the destructive mistake of falling head over heels, both times the people who so willingly shared that love sailing off into the wide blue yonder and never coming back. After the second trauma, two months ago, I put up the shutters on my heart and emotions, and decided to ride out the remainder of this shambles in sanity. For a while this worked just fine. What I hadn't bargained for was the arrival of a gentle, oh-so-considerate Australian named Ian Cameron."

There was a pause in the flow here, but I said nothing. There had to be more.

"No, there was no love affair as such. I fought that one all the way. Oh, how I fought it. Twice was enough for me and, as an observer at this place, I have no illusions about the precarious lifestyle in which you are all engaged. Then again, if you must know, I did like Ian very much. We were good friends, put it that way."

Now we both sat back for a minute and sipped the drinks.

"All right, Judy," I agreed, "what precisely do you want to know?"

"Just what exactly did you mean by 'hit'?" she asked. I could almost feel her wince as she framed the query.

Now, there was a direct question. If I waffled the answer, I could end up doing more harm than good, so I plonked for the blunt truth.

"It was one of those rare moments over a target, Judy, staring exclusively at another bomber for no particular reason. I had been caught in the middle of a whole lot of my own little disasters. The Mid-upper had

170

been hit; the plane had been hit; our aerials were all shot away. I think I simply glanced out of the window to try to escape."

"And ..." came the impatient push-on, as I hesitated for a bit.

Here we go, I thought.

"It was a direct hit, Judy. My candid opinion, for what it's worth, is that the crew felt no pain. And before you ask that next question, if one freak parachute did blossom clear, then I certainly didn't see it."

We both fell silent.

The truth had been flushed out; the hopeless yearning and clinging to the unknown had been laid to rest.

After a much longer pause this time, I had to come back in.

"I'm on the Battle Order tomorrow," I reminded Judy gently, "so I'll have to get off to bed. I'll get you another drink."

"No, don't do that." The WAAF officer image was gradually reasserting itself. "I'm off to bed, too. I'm the one assigned to give you all the intelligence angle tomorrow at briefing."

As we started to turn at the top of the stairs, one left and the other right, there was a hesitation.

"I'm so sorry, Judy."

"Oh, we were just good friends," she braved it out as she turned away quickly. "Good night."

"Good night."

I was grateful that I didn't have to witness the scene on the far side of that lady's bedroom door.

Maybe one day I would find the answer to that puzzling and perplexing question: Just how often is it possible to piece a broken heart together again?

CHAPTER
SIX

We Want Our Bombs Back

All fascination and apprehension, we had watched the fighter sort out its tactical moves. It had come out of the sun, fast and business-like, making a wide sweeping circle around R-Roger as it locked on to the bomber, like a shark sizing up its victim before the fatal attack.

Then, right on cue, its pilot had pulled his plane back, upward, and over to one side, now hanging 1,000 feet above us in a rear quadrant. It was the classic position from which to launch an attack. All three of our gun turret operators — front, upper and rear — had monitored the plane's every move, sweeping around as it had circled around, locking infra-red gun sights onto the outline of the fighter. The built-in technology then took care of the deflection and the wind factors. The stand-off was complete.

"Thank goodness it's one of ours," chipped in our Engineer.

"I'll go along with that." I added my thankfulness to Frank's, my eyes never leaving the fighter, now poised and ready to come boring down on our Lancaster. It was one of the latest Mark clipped-wing Spitfires, and its pilot and I had already completed the required let's-get-organised chit-chat. We were the main players in the fighter affiliation set-to, a confrontation that had been arranged about an hour before.

"Better go air test R-Roger," Squadron Leader Bass had suggested first thing in the morning, as soon as I had rounded the Flight Room door. "Maintenance reckon it's all patched up and ready to go."

Our Flight Commander was aware that we were on the Battle Order later in the day, and that Roger was our assigned assault wagon. In yesterday's fracas over Duisburg, poor old Roger had been peppered by enemy shrapnel. Luckily, no serious structural damage had been done. An air test was mandatory before a rejuvenated bomber would be cleared for further operational flying. Both on the ground and aloft, we would test everything relevant to our aircrew category.

"Test shouldn't take long," reckoned our boss, "so you can do some fighter evasion practice while you're up there. I've already arranged for all gun turrets on R-Roger to be fitted with cine cameras, and the attack plane should be with you in about an hour from now. Hang around the Wash area at twelve thousand feet. Don't bother to look for the fighter; he'll find you. Have fun!"

As I departed the Flight Room with the required courtesy salute, I got much the same knowing, mischievous grin from Squadron Leader Bass as I had seen on the face of Flight Lieutenant Smith a few months before. As pilots, they were both well aware that when it got down to hard-core corkscrewing — friendly or otherwise — about the only participants enjoying the gyrations would be the pilots.

The Spitfire turned lazily onto its side, hung there deliberately on a wingtip for what seemed an eternity, and then came boring in on the bomber like a hawk out of hell, executing a wide scything curve as it dived.

It was show time.

"Rolling over on a corkscrew . . ." I warned, with a slight pause while I got the timing just right, "now!"

The pilot of the Spitfire was making his initial attack a conventional one from the starboard side, so I hammered in full right rudder to narrow his angle, pushed the control column way forward, and turned the wheel to starboard to follow the rudder. Roger dropped out of the sky like a bag of wet cement. I was following the teachings of Kiwi Smudger Smith to the letter.

"Don't piss around," Smudge had tutored. "Carry out every manoeuvre to the limit — every turn, every dive, every climb. Give the wanker in the fighter a really distressing, withering time; one he'll recall over and over to his grandchildren."

How could any pupil fail to react to such eloquence?

My patter over the internal intercom was relentless. "Down starboard, rolling, down port, rolling, up port, rolling, up starboard". How I wished our Lancaster, R-Roger, could have spoken up for itself. After having been shot up and messed around over the Third Reich many times, this bomber, I could almost guarantee, was having the time of its cotton-picking life.

Which, alas, was more than I could say for the members of its crew. Gerry admitted that he had come close to losing his breakfast during the last bout of corkscrewing, and Clin, in the rear turret, said his blood ran cold when he saw the Lancaster's wings bend and wave in the extreme flying conditions.

Just as the attacks by the fighter varied continually, so, too, did my corkscrewing. The fighter pilot obviously approved. He flew alongside before departing, gave an elaborate thumbs-up, and did two beautiful slow rolls as he headed off for home.

There was no thumbs-up from any member of the crew. The fighter affiliation exercise very definitely hadn't made their day. As things turned out later in the afternoon, we discovered that there were many ways to spoil a day.

No two target set-to's were ever the same. Cologne, sitting just a little to the south of Happy Valley, and one of Germany's most important road, rail and water hubs, must have proved this point many times over the years to the pilots of Bomber Command. As the Reich's fifth city and originator of that famous perfumed toilet water, it was about to do so again.

The deception this time was the lead-in. It was perfect. Briefing had gone without a hitch: start-up was poetry, every engine firing as soon as Frank hit the button; and that taxi run along the perimeter track to the threshold of the runway-in-use was a scene that got to me every time. A string of fully laden Lancaster bombers weaving their deliberate pathway to glory was a spectacle that, once this war was over, would most likely never come again. Even the weather was riding thc rainbow.

"Jeez, that's a beautiful day," our Engineer told no one in particular. "I hope some stupid dick doesn't come along and ruin it."

"Just as long as we don't have to do any more corkscrewing," Clin got in the jab from his rear turret, "I don't care who comes along."

"I'll say 'Amen' to that one." Gerry must have felt he had to support the cause.

There was no more reaction but I got an elaborate wink from Frank.

All was clear from deck level to sky-blue infinity, the sun coming through the perspex windows all warm and soothing.

"Wonder if they'd notice," questioned a not-too-serious Frank, "if we didn't turn up at all for this caper? I'm sure the other 600 Lancasters could manage things quite well without us."

"We're one of the Gee-H leaders this time, Frank," I reminded our Engineer. "The two bombers hanging on to our wingtips might be a touch annoyed if we took off in a cloud of dust and small stones."

Frank shrugged that one off.

"They could come too." He was smiling as he stared through the front window at yet another scene that, in the not too distant future, would surely never come again. There were Lancaster bombers filling the sky ahead of Roger for as far as we could see; some streaming vapour off their wingtips, some not, depending on the operational height they had been allotted. We were flying at 20,500 feet.

"You're just trying to deprive those maidens and their anti-aircraft guns of their fun, Frank." The parting aside was from Jack, maps spread out before him in the Air Bomber's nose compartment. He was the eyes of the Navigator. While Gerry plotted and drew in our progress on his charts, Jack confirmed the bomber's positions with actual map references. Should a careless piece of shrapnel ever take our Navigator out of contention, the Air Bomber was the one who would slide onto the Navigator's seat and take over the navigation of the plane.

The French coast, the front line, the bomb line; these markers had all passed below R-Roger's flight progress. Gone now was the flippant repartee. The deeper we edged into enemy territory, the greater the danger of attack by German fighters, especially the infamous Messerschmitt 262 jets. They were so fast that they were all but impossible for our fighter cover to match.

Even the beautiful day was losing its appeal. Just as we had an uninterrupted view of the ground, so, too, did the German ground gunners have a perfect sighting of the bomber stream. They didn't have to feel for their adversary through layers of cloud cover. Each box of four ack-ack shell bursts could be seen by the gunners, and any errors of positioning corrected quickly, ensuring maximum discomfort for the bombers.

"This is gonna be one bugger of a target," lamented the Mid-upper Gunner while we were still well back from the holocaust. "All these friggers have got to do is to keep pumping up the shells. They can hardly miss."

The airspace above Cologne was indeed foreboding. One of my pet aversions, the myriad black plumes of smoke left behind by past explosions, were hanging there like gravestones; a blasphemy against the brilliant blue sky around them. But, as Ivor had warned, while the by-products of past explosions can cause concern, it was the current ones that could kill.

We were still on the outer fringes of the city when a unique piece of bad news filtered through. Courtesy of our radio, we were told that the Gee-H stations had gone out of commission. It was a breakdown that immediately put two-thirds of the Lancaster bomber stream out of action. Of the 600 bombers scheduled for the operation, 400 of them were from 3 Group.

As we were to learn later, the cut in radar service to the stream was an interruption that lasted a mere six to ten minutes but, as fate would have it, these were the vital six to ten minutes when the planes were over the target. Without Gee-H our bombing technique was rendered useless.

"Couldn't we just slash the bombs off using our own bomb sight?" questioned our Rear Gunner voicing a perfectly fair question, one with which I'm sure most of the aircrews hanging above Cologne at the time agreed. "If we drift a little bit off the aim line," Clin continued his plug, "I won't say anything, if you don't."

Harry was standing beside me on the flight deck now, and he was shaking his head vigorously.

"There's more to the signal, Skip." Our radio man was holding the message in his hand. "We have been ordered to ditch the Cookie in the North Sea, but they want all of those 15 × 500-pounders back at Stradishall."

"Bomber going down ahead, Phil." Jack's more urgent piece of news cut through the side talk. "Looks bad, and if he doesn't ditch his load fast, it'll get worse."

The Air Bomber in the injured Lancaster must have agreed, because we saw a string of 500-pounders drop out of its bomb bay like well drilled soldiers, followed by the ungainly cavortings of the notorious Cookie.

We had no more time to monitor someone else's grief. Bedlam and menace were filling our own world just outside the window. The smells, the smoke, the noise, the sweat, the incessant bombardment from below; all of these things were crowding in on the incredible situation now developing for the machines of 3 Group. Here we were, poncing like lollipops across one of the most lethal pieces of airspace on earth, and base had put up the shutters. Don't bomb. Bring those 500s back to base.

"Christ, Jack." I was both annoyed and fearful at the same time. "This is a dinger of a dilemma. Just look at the flak all over the place out there. All we need, all any one of these bombers needs, is for one shard of shrapnel to nobble a blockbuster and at least seven of us will get the chop, very rapidly."

"Orders are orders, Phil." Our Air Bomber was, of course, right.

"Your worst nightmare just came true behind us, Skip." Clin was the informant from the rear turret. "Lancaster blew up like a bloody Roman candle. There's no way the crew would feel anything."

"Did you acknowledge that radio message, Harry?" cut in a scheming Engineer, his glance brimming with devious intent.

Even before our wireless man answered, I was shaking my head.

"Acknowledge or not, Frank," I had to hold on to some sanity, "we can't whack through a direct order. I know our radio receiver could be out, or maybe the transmitter, but they would assum . . ."

Harry cut through the trivia.

"Of course I answered the signal." He was looking at and reacting to our Engineer's question. "I did that more or less on reflex."

We were flush over Cologne now and here and there I could see that the front Gee-H planes were losing height. This was all the encouragement I needed. Change flight levels and we would immediately give the ground gunners a harder time. They would have to reset their coordinates.

"To hell with this comedy, Gerry," I was warning the Navigator. "Whether or not Gee-H comes on again, I'm getting the hell out of this place, and I'm losing height right now."

"You're safe, Skip." The Navigator was resigned. "Gee-H couldn't do much good now."

"More grief behind us, Skip," said Clin, "but I'll save the detail for later."

"You have to wonder what's so sacred about Cologne," mused Frank, his head twisting in all directions as he looked for trouble with black crosses painted on their wings. "Our leaders weren't so touchy about Dresden."

No one answered that one, but it was a point to ponder.

"Same old deal." I had to go through the spiel yet again, wiping the sweat of both palms on my trouser legs. "Everyone who can, rubber neck everywhere. We'd be mad as hell if some frigger jumped us now, especially while we're loaded up with that garbage in the bomb bay."

Fifteen minutes later, with tempers and blood pressure settling down a pinch, Ivor said it out loud for us all.

"Nearly 3,000 aircrew in about 400 planes," complained our Mid-upper, "have just risked their lives over an enemy target for bugger all."

"Fair comment, Blondie," I had to admit, "but spare some thought for your pilot. They want me to put our friend, Roger here, back on the deck with 15 × 500-pounders still hanging in the straps. If just one of these ding-dongs explodes, it could alter our whole way of life."

The boys waited for it. I waited for it. Our Mid-upper always had the last word.

"Ah well," Ivor finalised. "It could add a bit of interest to things."

"All that aside," I felt it only fair to warn the boys, "if we get jumped by a fighter on the way back home, I'm getting shot of that Cookie faster than fast, no matter where we are. In a corkscrew, those 500-pounders will be enough for Roger to handle."

"Thinking back on what you said earlier about Dresden, Frank" — I had been niggling that one over — "I reckon there's been a bit of kick back on that attack, and our leaders are shying away from any more adverse comment. If we'd demolished Cologne Cathedral, there could have been meltdown in the public relations stakes. It took them hundreds of years to put it there. As you know, the Dresden attack didn't faze me. Having stood by and watched the Germans crucify Amsterdam, London, Manchester and Coventry, any measure of retribution we can filter back is just fine by me."

With the blockbuster ditched in the North Sea, and the 500s still aboard, we were just marginally below the maximum all-up weight for landing.

"You got away with it, Skip." Our Engineer seemed much happier when we were running along our home runway. R-Roger couldn't comment, but I bet our Lancaster was equally relieved.

CHAPTER
SEVEN

Too Easy, Too Fast

You can never tell with questions, they come in so
many different styles. Most are innocent and routine,
some are even throw-away, and then we have the glass
ones, questions so brittle that a careless answer can
shatter the consequences all over your head. The trick is
to recognise a delicate question when it comes along. I
had just recognised one.

"D'you think the singer and the song there are trying
to tell me something?"

Judy Melville asked the question. That, I thought, is
a query that should be allowed to mature for a bit,
hopefully long enough for me to come up with the
correct answer. The pair of us were having drinks in
the bar at the Mess. The message flowing through the
radio from the singer and the song boomed into our
here and now. The sad message declared:

> "I fall in love too easily
> I fall in love too fast;
> I fall in love so terribly hard
> For love to ever last.

My heart should be well schooled,
It's been fooled in the past;
But still, I fall in love too easily,
I fall in love too fast."

I looked across at Judy. Here was a perfectly charming, somewhat reticent lady who had paid the price for playing tag with this thing called love. Once the question had been asked, there followed a rueful expression, backed by a fragile smile. Both the expression and the smile seemed to beg for a straight answer. Now would not be a good time for frivolity.

"If you're accusing yourself of falling in love too fast," I answered, "then I'd say you were being a wee bit unfair. In addition to lots of other things, this war is a thief. It steals everything and anything it can lay its hands on. It steals our youth, barely giving us time to wave it goodbye. It steals our time, forcing us to hustle our lives along, including the delicate business of falling in love. And finally, the war steals even the people we cherish, brushing them aside like fallen autumn leaves.

"Even the sanctity of love itself is forced to speed up. Everyone is hoping that the war will leave their valuable dreams alone, knowing full well that the chopper is poised and ready to drop at any time. You didn't fall in love too fast, Judy. You just fell in love. It was the war that was moving too fast."

If the ballad on the radio was trying to push the message over on to someone, then maybe he had better pick on me. Judy and I seemed to get along together like a dream. Even after meeting only a few times, we

185

were free and easy in each other's company. I found myself looking forward to meeting her, going out of my way to find her, wishing I could spend more and more time in her company. I was oblivious to everything around when she was near, aware that Judy could make even the cold and rainy days seem fantastic. As all of these indicators dropped into place, I knew very well that it was my heart, and not Judy's, that could be falling in love too easily, too fast.

It was rather sad because the beautiful lady across the table had already made her position clear. The shutters were up. Judy would hardly welcome the idea of tangling yet again with someone in operational flying.

"Thank you, Philip, for not laughing at my question. Let's go for a walk along the river. It's a beautiful evening."

"A perfectly wonderful idea," I had to admit. "Now I can see why they made you an intelligence officer."

Judy gave me one of her whimsical, side-angle glances, smiling and pushing me toward the exit as she did so. Our thoughts, hopes, jokes and pleasures seemed to skip on ahead of us. We were happy to be in each other's company. I could tell that we felt safe, one with the other, and yet . . . and yet . . . what were those unknowns, those shadows fringing along the edge of our world?

Slowly, ever so slowly, as we walked quietly along by the river's edge, truth tiptoed in from those shadows. It was a truth helped along first by a finger seeking one of my fingers, and then by a hand lacing positively into mine. It was a truth confirmed when Judy called me "Peter" by mistake, quite unaware that she had done so. Peter, as I discovered along the way, was the name of the fighter pilot whom Judy had loved and lost in Scotland. Ah, the intricacies and depths of true love.

I may well have been the physical character pacing along that country pathway, but I was sure Judy was holding tightly to another hand at another time, a hand that had been wrenched ruthlessly from hers to the heartless symphony of chattering cannon fire and exploding ack-ack shells. I was merely the surrogate, helping to heal a broken heart, nothing more.

Now there was a shattering truth. Who, I wondered, would be on hand to heal the bruises on my heart? Judy must have decided to help out, coming back from her reverie to the world around us.

"And how is your war coming along these days, Flight Lieutenant Gray?" she asked in mock formality.

"Well now, Judy, we could have a choice situation here." I was waffling a bit. "Lately, there have been good bits, and there have been bad bits."

"Let's get rid of one of the baddies first," our intelligence officer suggested. "Wheel out some of the grief."

"All right," I agreed, "how about a major mistake for starters. I pulled off a blunder yesterday that has been niggling and punching away at my conscience ever since. Of course you realise that this admission could ruin my reputation in your eyes; admitting to a mistake, just when you thought I was perfect."

Judy smiled, tilted her head back, raised her eyes to the sky. But she said not a word. My saga was allowed to roll on.

"You must have read through the reports of yesterday's bash on Heligoland. It's a rock island stuck way out in the North Sea. There were 720 bombers. The chance of serious fighter opposition was minimal. It was a cinch. All we had to do was stay in the air and get there. Then the ball started to roll downhill; at least it did for us. Twenty minutes from base the starboard outer engine began to lose interest."

"Frank, our Engineer, checked the fuel contents and levers. Everything was in order. The hitch had to be with a fuel pump, a valve, or a line rupture somewhere. The oil pressure began to drop while the oil temperature was rising. Soon the engine was running rough. Either we cut the engine fast or the whole unit would start to fry and catch fire. It was decision time and I'm almost sure I made the wrong one.

"Oh, it was a safe decision. In fact, if you felt like being a little unkind, you could say it was the 'chicken' decision. I closed the engine down, feathered the prop into wind, and pulled out of the stream. We were on our way back to base.

"As soon as I hit the deck, and non-stop since then, the questions have been hammering and screaming away at me. Why did I pull away from the stream? Why didn't I just close the engine down and carry on with the three good ones? What was the great problem? True, we would probably have been one of the last planes to reach the target, and maybe 15,000 feet

188

would be the best height we could reach with the load, but I still don't think there would have been all that much opposition to worry about. Maybe the enemy fighters could have singled us out, but there is every chance that some of our own fighter umbrella would have come to our aid. I blew it."

"Just for the record," Judy wanted to know, "what did you do with the bombs you were carrying?"

"Funny you should ask that, because here at least we were on familiar ground. We had to bring back fifteen 500-pounders from the Cologne attack. That time, of course, most of the petrol had been used up on the trip to the Ruhr and back, so we were able to land — very carefully I admit — back on the runway with the fifteen bombs still on board."

"This time, on the Heligoland attack, the load was a boomer: eight 500-pounders, and eight 1,000-pounders plus most of the petrol still in the tanks. There was no way we could land back at base with that lot. There we were, like lollipops, having to jettison 12,000 pounds of beautiful bombs into the Wash area, just off our east coast."

Judy could sense depression starting to creep in on the scene.

"All right," she said, as brightly as she could, "now let's have one of the good bits. You did say there were some of those, didn't you?"

Now we were both smiling again.

"How about a secret then?" I said. "Surely that's got to be one of the best bits."

I could see Judy's eyes starting to brighten up and sparkle straight away, reinforcing yet again one of the great facts of life. From nine to ninety, all girls love secrets.

"Tell me more," she said, a squeeze of the hand confirming her interest.

"Two days ago I shot over to the Stores Section, the tailor there having promised to sew the second rings on the sleeves of my uniform and greatcoat. The finishing touches were still being applied when I got there, so I browsed around the place for a bit. That was when I stumbled across the secret. The Stores people were busily engaged in another and much more ambitious sewing job. Huge sheets of canvas were being pieced together into what looked like huge hammocks or panniers. When I asked what these mysterious pieces of canvas were to be used for, all I got was a shrug. 'No idea,' replied the people on the machines, 'but they're certainly meant to fit into the bomb bay of a Lancaster, three panniers to a bomber.'"

I gave a quizzical glance in Judy's direction.

"Any ideas? After all, you're one of the intelligence officers."

Like all good intelligence officers, Judy was apparently thinking about both the answer and the possible implications. Certainly there had been no quick denial, meaning that she did know something.

"Creeping along the conspiratorial tentacles of the grapevine," my companion admitted in somewhat measured wording, "I did indeed hear something about food drops from the air. What I have not been able to

190

discover is to whom the food will be dropped, and by which aircraft. Since you have seen our Stores personnel beavering away at the panniers, then it would seem that our own Lancasters will carry out the drops. Intriguing, isn't it?"

"Certainly is," I agreed, "and it will make a pleasant change, dropping life and hope rather than death and destruction."

What I would rather have told Judy was that I found her much more intriguing than any canvas panniers, but something made me shy away from that one. Our walk continued, the chatter brightening up quite a bit, but my thoughts kept drifting back to that song on the radio. A sort of contented silence dropped in around us.

While the war, fate, and red-hot shrapnel were busy disposing of the objects of Judy's love and affections, I had been plodding along the way. Now that I had caught up, and was discovering my own affection for this beautiful, elegant lady, alas, it was too late. Her heart was already on "hold".

The singer, the song, and the lyrics had indeed been offered for me. This time around, I had fallen in love too easily; I had fallen in love too fast.

CHAPTER
EIGHT

The Big One

Only yesterday, or was it a few weeks ago, we had been the new boys on the Squadron; one operational flight to our credit, and the reputation for pulling off suicidal leaps over hangars. Today, we were becoming very good at our business.

We returned several times to the same targets, identities blurring as the cities, oil depots, tactical targets, harbours, coking plants and railway marshalling yards passed by 20,000 feet below.

Our credits were mounting ... Wesel, Wesel, Gelsenkirchen, Kamen, Gelsenkirchen, Gelsenkirchen, Cologne, Gelsenkirchen, Datteln.

Each name in that line-up had been a living, thriving home town for the thousands of people who walked wide across its bustle and beauty every day. Each target may have been just another chopping block for Bomber Command, but it was the end of the rainbow for its owners and citizens.

As our list of operations grew longer, the mood changed. On the first few runs over enemy territory, we considered it a miracle to squeeze through the atrocity and rage that was an enemy target, and stagger back to base. It was a thrill to see our names on the notice-boards all over the airfield, one of the élite list of crews to grace the legendary Battle Order. Later, custom and expertise clouded this perspective. We accepted the outrageous idea that we were fireproof, and possibly bombproof and bulletproof into the bargain. This was a vanity that manifested itself just before take-off, while we were still marking time at the Lancaster dispersal pad.

As we fooled around with the ground crew, the Lancaster all armed and bombed-up ready to go, we would also be armed — with pieces of chalk, the joke being to scatter obscene messages all over the casings of the 500-pound bombs and the 4,000-pound block-buster. The real hike was our own personal and arrogant message, taunting fate outrageously.

Sometimes this personal claim would be in its abbreviated form, "GACB"; other times the theme would be written out in full — "Gray Always Comes Back". Such insolence should have provoked fate and screwed our destiny into the concrete. It was obvious that moderation and the arrogance of our unthinking youth had absolutely nothing in common. These were the early days.

As the battle raged on, including the two alien excursions into the night skies over Kiel harbour, destiny began to kick back with a few tricks of its own, cutting our truculent selves down to size. Several times during these hazardous affairs above the Ruhr Valley, and over Kiel, we had come close indeed to being zeroed right out of the game. The message to us was being underlined.

Even with Lady Luck on our shoulders, we could only expect her to shake down so many favours in our direction. The big chop was just a careless piece of red hot shrapnel away.

The Battle Order was on the boards by the time Judy and I left the bar. It was a boomer, the most ambitious we had seen since arriving at Stradishall. Every spare crew and aircraft on the Squadron had been pulled into service. The Wing Commander removed the curtain from the blackboard, delivering the punchline as he did so.

"The target for this afternoon, gentlemen, is Essen. The effort will be maximum, using a thousand bombers: one thousand and fifty-four to be precise." The announcement sent a buzz around the crowded room.

There had been one, possibly two, raids of this magnitude in the past, but this was our first thousand-bomber operation.

Essen was within the precinct of Happy Valley. Its anti-aircraft protection and fighter cover were legendary. This was a city chock-a-block with heavy industry, the most important of which was the massive armaments complex owned by the Krupp family. In addition to the German citizens employed by Alfred Krupp, a reputed 70,000 forced labourers had been brought in from occupied countries.

Bomber Command had visited Essen many times in the past, paying a cruel price for venturing over the many muzzles of its practised and highly skilled anti-aircraft units. This time it was the description of the attack that took us all by surprise. Despite the fact that Essen was bristling with top priority targets, the WingCo ignored the reality.

"This time, gentlemen," he told us, "we are to look upon the entire city as a tactical target." "Any questions?"

Bombing by the Command was an activity that rolled on relentlessly day and night. As the pawns of the moment, we piled into the transport which would wheel us out to the Lancasters.

One particular WAAF driver used to fascinate all of us. Her back-chat with the boys, indeed anyone who came within range of her wagon, was non-stop and laced with a stream of four-letter Anglo-Saxon terms that could curl your hair. Perhaps the fact that this maiden was also petite and quite a looker added to the surprise when she cut loose with her colourful chatter.

There may have been another side to this story. This driver had been transporting aircrews to and from bombers for quite a while. She knew many of us well, one or two of the boys personally and very well. This WAAF driver also knew that the shuttle run to the Lancaster was the last run on earth for many of the crews. She invariably brought back fewer people from the dispersals than she had originally sent on their way. Behind the wall of invective, this lady was possibly hiding some of her own private fears and sadness.

"Starboard inner," I instructed, and so the real show got on its way one more time.

From our elevated position up front in the Lancaster, Frankie pointed out the engine to the ground crew clustered around the static battery trolley below. Thumbs-up were exchanged from both sides of the operation, and then the Engineer pressed the starter button for the appropriate Merlin engine. And so it went: port inner, port outer, starboard outer, until all four engines were growling and flexing their muscles.

"Bomb doors closed," was my next suggestion. Frank pulled up the lever, locking it into place. All of our chalked-up messages to the citizens of Essen and the Nazi hierarchy in general were now sealed away in the 33-foot bomb bay. There was little chance that the people at deck level would ever read our basic advice. The high explosive content of the carriers would spread them over the local landscape.

The ground crew disconnected the umbilical cord which had been supplying power from the battery trolley to the plane, flashing the familiar thumbs-up to point out that the Lancaster now had to take care of all services with its own power. The ground crew completed its immediate part of the action by marshalling us safely from the parking circle towards the exit.

The snaking, curving taxi line moving inexorably towards the runway threshold was a scene at that moment being repeated on airfields all over England. One by one we moved into the dramatic starter position at the beginning of the concrete, blasting up the four engines ready for the all-or-nothing take-off charge down the long runway. Until I could ease our heavy load of petrol, bombs and plane ever so gently off the deck, I'm sure I even stopped breathing for a time. Finally we climbed up to take our chances over the Third Reich for the tenth time.

The American Flying Fortresses were also preparing for another target, their forming-up procedure going on overhead as we took off. There was a marked difference in the two approaches to launching an attack, the US Army Air Corps affair being something akin to a replay of the Fourth of July. The Royal Air Force used the stream principle, and could carry on directly from the runway to join the long line of bombers already making their way towards Germany. Staggering the take-off times locked everyone into the correct place in the stream, thereby saving valuable petrol and time. It was all done with the minimum of fuss.

The American system was based on firepower. They formed up in large 36-ship "Vs". Bringing these unwieldy clusters of planes into being was a major task, providing quite a show.

The front men — the leader planes — would become airborne and circle designated anchor spots here, there and everywhere. Each leader would then poop off dozens of allotted colour flares, be it green, red, blue, yellow or whatever. Pre-briefed, the other thirty-five Fortresses in a specific formation would then shoot skywards at intervals, hooking up to the leader plane pooping off its colour. This exercise could go on for up to an hour before the impressive armada of multiple 36-ship formations finally nosed around and headed towards Germany, their petrol tanks now somewhat depleted.

Theory would suggest that the firepower from just one of these formations of thirty-six Flying Fortresses would be devastating. Maybe so, but that didn't stop them from getting punched out of the sky in large numbers.

Then there was the matter of night bombing. Obviously a 36-ship formation was impossible to hold together in the dark, so individual Fortresses had to go it alone on a night operation. Somehow, this didn't seem to work out very well. The United States Army Air Corps (USAAC) did indeed carry out a few night operations in their early days in the European Theatre of Operations (ETO), but this gambit was quickly abandoned. The Royal Air Force and her other allies continued to operate day and night.

By now, all the planes in our own gigantic armada advancing toward the Ruhr were at their bombing height. The 154 Lancasters from our 3 Group were at the rear of the stream, meaning that we had 900 bombers from 1, 4, 5, 6 and possibly more Groups stretched out ahead of us.

From our privileged front-row seats in the cabin of R-Roger, Frank and I could see bombers stretching before us literally to our distant horizon, the remainder having already passed out of sight. With the careless acceptance of youth, I doubt if we fully realised the significance of the scene we were favoured to witness: over one thousand bombers advancing on a single target.

Viewed from friendly ground level, the vision must have been awe-inspiring as the seemingly endless stream of heavy bombers passed relentlessly on its way. Viewed from enemy territory at ground level, the whole spectacle would be petrifying, a display of aerial might to strike fear into the staunchest hearts. Unbelievably, our numbers were to be boosted even higher as we crossed the Belgian coastline.

At three degrees east, somewhere around Ostend, the bomber stream was joined by its protective fighter cover, the numbers in this mobile shield being relative to the number of bombers in the stream. With an attack of this magnitude, the maximum number of fighters would be used, although they would link up with the flow of heavy machines at intervals. That way, the fighters would spread themselves along the stream. Our little friends, as the fighters were referred to by their four-engined cousins, had a limited petrol capacity and could spend less time in the air. Besides, there was little point in their riding shotgun when we were in friendlier skies.

There must have been hundreds of Spitfires, Lightnings, Hurricanes and Mustangs dispersed along the whole length of the bomber stream. They usually flew about 10,000 feet above us at 30,000 feet. Since our cruising speed was much lower than theirs, the fighter pilots would be bored out of their parachutes with this "minder" duty. The chiefs were aware of this tedium angle, and had a bonus built in for them.

Once our little friends had seen us through the target area and we were all pointed for home, they were free to scythe down from their 30,000-foot guard height to deck level, zeroing in on the patchwork scene like a swarm of locusts on a day off. They were still well inside enemy territory, so their instruction brief was simple: "If it will be profitable to the enemy war effort, and it moves — hit it." With their guns hanging heavy with bullets, and their cannons chocked up with shells, these fighters must have felt relieved when they finally got down to zero feet, low-levelling across the German countryside as fast as their wings would carry them. It would have been dangerous even to blink while these single-engine marauders were passing by.

Our immediate concern, though, was Essen. Our part of the stream was now just twenty minutes short of the drop point. The 900 Halifax and Lancaster bombers must have been starting their churn through the massacre and inferno of the target while we tail-enders were still on the approach, spreading "Window" over the countryside.

Window was the code name given to strips of metalled paper, yet one more tool used in the never-ending radar war. The basic principle of radar is that a radio signal is transmitted, bounces off whatever object it hits, and echoes back to receivers capable of collecting the returning signals. Both sides were working hard in this area to gain an advantage, but the British radar scientists were always ahead of their German counterparts in the use of this medium.

Enemy early warning radar equipment had no difficulty picking up the presence of hostile planes approaching their valuables, allowing them to alert their defences. So, thought the devious British scientists, why not give the people monitoring the German radar screens some early warnings that would really space them out. After all, the radio signals themselves were neutral, quite happy to bounce back off whatever object presented itself. Experiments proved that the signal appearing on a cathode ray tube was much the same for a Lancaster bomber as it was for a small piece of metalled paper. There was only one way to go.

Large quantities of metalled paper were produced, cut into strips, and wrapped into small, manageable bundles. Bombers were fitted with chutes leading to atmosphere from the air bomber's nose compartment. Around twenty minutes before a target, or when dictated at briefing, the air bomber would start to drop a steady supply of this "Window" through the chute.

The initial results, as German records have shown, were electrifying. On enemy radar monitoring screens, what had been approaching as a substantial but routine hostile bomber stream suddenly became a veritable horde of bombers descending on the hapless Reich. Distress, approaching chaos and panic, rocked through the system, the fighter groups, ack-ack commanders and defence planners trying desperately to dream up some way to cope with this new and apparently limitless swarm of planes.

It was a distress, of course, that lasted one, possibly two days at most. Mysterious slivers of silver paper were spread across the German landscape like confetti, turning up in suburban back yards, city streets, country lanes, military establishments — everywhere. But then, discovery of the truth is one matter; coping with the phenomenon was something else.

Flak was always our greatest concern. The vulgarity of spent and exploding ack-ack shells was already spreading its grief as we confronted the challenge of this bombing run.

"It never gets any easier, does it?"

Frank made the observation from his fold-out seat next to mine, his words directed more to the uncaring world around him than to me in particular.

"Nope," I replied anyway, though neither of us took our mesmerised gaze off the confusion and disorder in front of us.

The other four bomber groups had been using their own technique of marking the place with Wanganui flares precision dropped by the Lancasters of the Pathfinder Force. While we were still a fair distance from the city, the calm voice of the Master Bomber could be heard issuing his ever-changing instructions. His radio chatter ceased as our end-of-the-line 3 Group attack got underway.

We would use the Gee-H radar system to drop our bombs, the aiming point being different from that covered by the 900 machines running ahead of us.

"Here we go again then." My warning at this point was working into a routine. "Everyone who can, watch out for any of these crafty bastards who may decide to creep up on us. Clin, Ivor, you're the main men covering our backs."

Acknowledgements rippled back over the RT from around Roger. Now the real danger of the anti-aircraft fire folded in about us. With the thumping and clumping at all levels, the same eerie, uneasy feeling began to creep up from the nape of my neck to the crown of my head. It was like waiting and bracing in the dark, unsure of the unknown lurking in the shadows. In fact, I was the one person in the Lancaster with positive protection in the back area. There was a steel shield behind my seat, all the way from the floor level to behind my head. That left plenty of space for bullets and shrapnel to cut in from under, over, or either side.

Just in case the opposition got lucky and cut me out of the game, we did have contingency plans. Frank knew how to release my seat straps, and would lift me out of the driver's seat. It was imperative that someone take control of the wheel and the rudder pedals as fast as possible. The danger of collision or being bombed from above was forever with us. Jack, having completed a fair part of the Wings course in Canada before being transferred to the course for air bombers, was the one who would have taken my place in an emergency.

As legend and record can prove, the rear turret in a bomber is one of the most dangerous places, the enemy fighters usually attacking that area from behind and below. To compensate for this danger, and at the request of our leaders, the makers of the Lancaster provided a mobile steel shield partially to protect the rear gunner. Attached to the framework of the rear turret, the piece of protective steel would rise or fall as the four Browning machine guns were elevated or depressed. That was the theory. Unfortunately, self-preservation and human nature elbowed out the theory.

As the shrapnel started to slice around uncomfortably close, and bullets and shells were becoming a danger to the gunner's health, a few simply elevated their four guns, thus also elevating the steel protective shield. That in place, the rear gunner could sit in behind it, much like the ostrich sticking its head in the sand. The operator's hope was that the war would go away and leave him alone. Things didn't work out that way. When our leaders realised the misdemeanour, they arranged for the pieces of protective half-inch steel to be removed from all rear turrets.

"Christ," Blondie was the first to see it, "A-Able's been hit. Looks bad. It's starting to go down."

Able was our next-door neighbour, we acting as its Gee-H leader. It was flying slightly behind us on the port side.

"Count the 'chutes if you get a chance," I suggested, glancing quickly out the port side window as I spoke.

As far as I could see, the big bomber had been caught amidships by a direct hit and was starting to buckle in the middle like a chocolate bar.

"I knew both the gunners in that crew." Clin's voice came forward from the rear turret over the RT, the tone both sad and shocked.

"So did I," chipped in Ivor from the upper turret.

"Bomb doors open."

Our routine went on regardless, but I knew the thought that was racing through our minds. The tiniest shift in the general flow of the stream, and ours would have been the bomber now spiralling ever faster on its final, dramatic plunge toward the deck.

"Watch M-Mike out to starboard, Skip!" The warning came from Clin. "It's drifting in a bit close."

"Thanks, Clin." I had a look. "I've got it."

"I wish these bastards wouldn't hang above us like that." Blondie sounded angry. "Way up there, they're fireproof. We're the stupid friggers down here who'll get hit if their air bomber presses the tit too early."

I eased Roger a bit more to port, but I couldn't spare much time staring skywards. We were now on the precision part of the bomb run. It was the plane dead ahead of us that was causing me grief. The pilot, obviously busy doing the spot-on flying bit, was unaware that he was falling back on to me. His slipstream, too, was starting to waffle us around. I could ease off my speed slightly, but I would then cause problems for the poor sod behind me. From his privileged position in the glass-fronted nose of the Lancaster, Jack was witnessing another disaster.

"A bomber up front in trouble, Phil," he said. "It was hit while its bomb doors were wide open."

This time I didn't dare ask Jack to look out for signs of parachutes. It didn't seem worthwhile. We ourselves were now poncing along with bomb doors open, our wares exposed for all the shrapnel in the world to see. I felt like shouting a plea to Jack over the RT: "For frig's sake, press that bloody button and let's get out of this

205

frigging death trap", but self-control prevailed. In due course, and not before, the good news came through.

"Bombs away."

R-Roger obviously liked the news too, bouncing about 500 feet upward as its lethal load fell away to cause more grief and pain to Essen. Now that over a thousand bombers had passed by, splattering yet another 13,000,000 pounds of anguish and agony over this high-profile industrial city of the Ruhr, its citizens must be having serious doubts about their thousand-year Reich.

Fifteen minutes later we watched with envy as Mustangs and Spitfires of our part of the protective screen broke formation, cut away individually from the swarm, and bulleted down through 30,000 feet toward the checkerboard layout below. For the next few minutes, even the butterflies would be in grave danger of annihilation.

In the more leisurely four-engine Lancaster we drank our coffee, lost height gently, but continued to cast a nervous eye into all corners of the hostile skies.

"I can tell you for nothing, Frank," I said, smiling across at the Engineer, "I'd be bloody mad if some evil bastard came along now and killed us, especially after we've just come through all that lot."

Other inner thoughts, though, were lingering back there with our squadron friends in poor old A-Able. Even if they had managed to parachute clear — and we hadn't seen any 'chutes open — there would be no sanctuary of a home base for them. As we slid through the low-level murk into the drizzle over the south of

England, I had Jack and Frank for company in the front cabin. In the middle of the general conversation of the moment, it seemed like a good time to slip in a little dash of philosophy.

"From what I've seen and read over the past few days, I reckon we're soon going to have to face a fact of life," I reflected. "We're rapidly running short of war."

CHAPTER
NINE

Just Routine

"You'll have to switch to U-Uncle, Gray." Squadron Leader Bass was trying to break the news gently. "Some nut, and I'm not going to trade names, released his bombs in R-Roger while — you'll have to believe this — the bomb doors were still closed! As a result, poor old Roger's underside is a bit damaged and dented."

Our Flight Commander grimaced and concluded, "Sorry about that. I know Roger was your favourite plane."

"Was there a Cookie aboard, Sir?" I asked, mentally cringing at the thought.

"No there was not." The boss was smiling now. "If there had been, neither Roger nor the crew would have felt any more pain, ever again."

And a little later . . .

"They did what?" Ivor cut loose in his louder than usual loud approach. Now it was my turn to pass on the bad news.

"We've been switched to U-Uncle," I continued. "It's a perfectly good plane. Of the four times we've visited Gelsenkirchen, Uncle's been with us twice."

That partially calmed things down, but the asides took a little longer to taper off.

"Forgot to open the bomb doors!" Jack was shaking his head in disbelief.

"That," chipped in Harry, "is like starving to death because you forgot to open your mouth."

As the day unfolded, our war became more than a little confused. By mid-forenoon, rumour had Heligoland as the target, but this had changed to Hamburg by noon. Come one o'clock there was an operational stand-down, whereupon Wing Commander Giles made plans for us to switch wars, turning to the sports field to achieve a double purpose: one, to occupy us in a healthy pursuit; and, two, to have his crews on hand just in case the War Council changed its mind and called for air support. Originally, no doubt, our genial Commander imagined he had simply arranged for us to play a game of cricket. As a Canadian, he didn't quite realise he had a tiger by the tail.

The make-up of 186 Squadron was, roughly, half Australian air-crews and half British, a set-up that had no great significance in itself providing everyone kept his mouth shut. That was like asking Bugsy Malone to stop eating cream doughnuts. No sooner was the serious cricket match under way than someone on the British side referred to the Australians as "these bloody Colonials". That did it! The game deteriorated quickly into "them" and "us". It was open war. Some of the bowling was vicious, the ball arriving at the batman's end at an assortment of heights and speeds. Batting and throwing was little better.

"Christ!" Flight Lieutenant Cowley was visibly relieved when his stint at the crease was over. "It's safer over an enemy target than it is out there."

Maybe next time the WingCo would go for baseball. As a Canadian, that's a game he understood. He did at least succeed in keeping us off the streets. After all, there didn't seem to be much point in starting World War Three while we were still trying to finish off number two.

Brushing all rumour aside, we discovered that the cricket had taken the place of what was to have been another thousand-bomber raid, or at least close to it. A stream with 976 aircraft was to be beamed toward Heligoland. Planning had been completed, the Battle Orders made ready for all relevant operational bomber stations, and Intelligence briefed and ready to roll. Met had stepped in and put up the shutters at the last minute.

No need to worry, though. Our leaders had a wide and wild assortment of targets to choose from.

"I bet they just close their eyes," reckoned Clin, "and throw a dart in the general direction of a map of the Third Reich. Wherever the arrow hits — 'target for today'."

As things turned out the next day, it was to be a target for tonight rather than one for the daylight hours. That was alien stuff for the daytime flyers of 186. I had done no flying at night for three months.

"Hope I still remember what to do in the dark," I said to no one in particular, and I meant it. This made the perfect opening for the ever-vigilant Harry.

"From what I've seen of you and that luscious piece of Waafery from Intelligence," reckoned our radio man, "I'd say you remembered very well what to do in the dark."

On the night, there was plenty of reaction and interest as the boss flicked the cover off the target board in the briefing room.

"Kiel, Gentlemen, is your target for tonight." The Wing Commander gave the initial details of this port on the Baltic Sea, placed approximately 100 kilometres north of Hamburg. "Geographically," the WingCo continued, "it's out on a limb of land, meaning that we can do quite a bit of flying over the North Sea before submitting ourselves to the agony of their ack-ack guns. To try to stay clear of their radar, our altitude on this leg will be 1,500 feet. That's low, and the water's not very far away, so be careful."

Other officers from Met, Armaments, Navigation and Intelligence came forward with their input. Take-off times would be between 2200 and 2210 hours, each bomber loaded with one blockbuster and twelve 500-pound bombs. Fuel load was 1,700 gallons, specific aiming points being warships and shore installations.

"There will be 584 bombers up there tonight," Wing Commander Flying concluded the briefing, "roughly half of them from 3 Group. True, our navigators have been given Gee-H coordinates but these should be used for bombing only in a back-up situation. Such an alternative would occur if the Master Bomber went off the air for one reason or another. As we know, these gentlemen live a somewhat tenuous existence around six to eight thousand feet above and around the target, and are prime marks for both ground gunners and enemy night fighters. Nevertheless, while they are active, they can see best how the attack is developing to obtain maximum effect. So, bomb visually on the target indicator flares if possible, obeying the instructions of the Master Bomber. These Wanganui flares come in beautiful shades of yellow, blue, red, green, and white, and crews like yourselves have risked their lives to dangle them over the target."

First leg was a long one way out over the North Sea, and the flight level was barely above circuit height. As the menace and gloom covering the water swallowed us up, the danger of the situation became clearer.

"This is tricky, Frank," I confided to the Engineer. "There are a lot of bombers out there thundering along the same course and at this same low altitude. Fifteen hundred feet doesn't give us much room to manoeuvre."

Nodding in agreement, Frank was already swivelling his head in all directions, seeking out trouble.

"And there's another boomer ahead." I had just thought of this one.

"What's that?" Frank continued to probe the gloom.

"Nearer we get to the enemy coast," I said, "the greater the danger there is of having enemy night fighters out looking for us. After all, even at this ridiculous height, I bet they've already picked us up on their radar. Six hundred bombers are very difficult to hide."

"Couldn't we start the climb early?" suggested a hopeful Engineer.

I was already shaking my head.

"Do that, Frank," I said, "and the radar behind us — ours — will pick us up. Our orders are: 'Hold 1,500 until crossing the enemy coast. Then climb up to bombing height.'"

Jack had joined us on the flight deck.

"I hate to add to any forebodings you two may have," he educated us, "but if we get into strife with another bomber at this flight level — enemy fighter, or whatever — don't even think about ditching the Cookie. Its blast, even at 1,500 feet, would have devastating consequences."

"One thing for sure," I added, "if an enemy fighter does appear, there's no way I can throw Uncle into a corkscrew at this height. It'll just have to be even-Stevens: our guns against his guns."

"Everyone who can," I advised over Uncle's intercom system, "keep a lookout in every direction. I've got to keep my eyes firmly fixed on this blind flying panel. Any glitch in our altitude, speed or direction at this flight level, and our war would come to an end very rapidly."

Then again, while we had forgotten all about Destiny, she had not forgotten about us. Fifteen minutes out on the long North Sea course, she struck.

Smoke! At least three of us smelt it at the same time and, as reason assures us, where there's smoke . . . Fire is one of the greatest fears in an operational aircraft. Sitting on 12,000 pounds of gunpowder and steel was one thing, but having a fire to warm it up was something else again.

"Where the hell's it coming from, Frank?" Ask and worry was about all I could do. The unflappable Harry, who had come out from behind his wireless sets, joined Jack and Frank on the flight deck. All three searched. I sweated.

"There it goes," pounced our Air Bomber, pointing at the back of one of Harry's radios. The Type 52 Resistance unit was on fire. Among them they used two fire extinguishers to subdue the flames, and I ordered Harry to switch off the set for good. There would be no more contact with base, but we could live without that.

During the excitement, and even to this day, I would have to admit that I haven't the slightest idea what a Type 52 Resistance unit looks like, or what function it serves. All I know is that, for a short time, it threatened to kill us all.

"Take my word for it, Skip," Harry had assured me at the time, "without it most of the radio services are buggered."

Happy thought, and the night was still young.

What I didn't know at that specific moment was that Frank was monitoring another private problem of his own. It would surface in due course.

Approaching the enemy coastline, U-Uncle moved us steadily from the lowly 1,500 feet to 20,000 feet, "George" doing most of the work. Uncle had just had its Mark III auto-pilot replaced by a Mark IV. This new model was beautiful, responding to climbs and turns at the flick of a wrist. All I had to do was lean forward and set the new course on the Dead Reckoning Compass repeater, and watch it all happen. In the event of possible collision or the presence of night fighters, "George", the automatic pilot, could be disengaged quickly.

By the time we reached Kiel, the now familiar mayhem and savagery were well underway. Target Indicator (TI) flares in brilliant clusters of red and green were dangling and shimmering over the city just as German citizens had described them — "like Christmas trees". The WingCo was right too; they did make a beautiful picture. Beautiful — but deadly.

While the target flares went down, very accurate and heavy ack-ack flak was coming back up. Blockbusters were erupting like mushrooms all over the dock area.

"Two enemy fighter flares starboard side, Skip." The warning came from the rear turret. That news kept everyone's ulcers on hold.

"Jeez, Frank," I imparted, aware that he could do nothing about it. "I wish I could stop the sweat from bubbling out of the palms of my hands. This bloody steering wheel is slithering all over the place."

We could hear the Master Bomber's authoritative patter in our headsets, so some of the radio's reception was still ticking over. Without the long-range signals from base, though, there had been no update on the wind.

"Lane coned in the searchlights up front, Skip," Ivor informed.

"I see him," I acknowledged, and was preparing for the final run when . . .

"Dive, Skip," from Ivor again, loud and urgent. Reflex had Uncle diving long before the rest of my mental parts caught up.

"Bloody hell," our Mid-upper almost screamed, "there's always got to be the comedian. Silly bugger was settling in on top of us."

Not daring to mention it, I could only imagine the problems such a sudden and violent dive must have had on Gerry. He would have pens, charts and instruments all over his navigation table.

Searchlights were probing everywhere, hoping to get lucky. The trick wasn't to run from them, but to turn toward the beam and flick through it quickly. Then again, while this manoeuvre would work for the white lights, there was no way to fool the blue ones. When these locked on to a bomber, they held on. With all this searchlight glare, plus the TIs, fires on the ground, explosions, photoflashes, fighter flares and spoofs, it was like Piccadilly Circus on a Friday night.

"'Bout a minute to go, Skip," came the warning from Gerry at the navigation table. I, and no doubt everyone else aboard, braced for the tension and torment of this meticulous part of the bomb run.

Jack was now more or less in charge.

"Hold it steady at that, Phil," as he started the final run-down.

We could hear the Master Bomber directing all air bombers to go for the green TIs. Accurate flying was now imperative, regardless of what was happening outside.

"Left a bit." "Bit more." "Steady." "Steady." "Bombs away!"

U-Uncle reared up in relief; just about the same time an ack-ack shell came a wee bit too close. None of its shards seemed to touch us. Now it was the 30-seconds-of-agony time, Uncle continuing to fly straight and level like a sitting duck.

This would be one helluva time for the gunners to pick up a night fighter, but that is exactly what they did. Leaving the air free, I listened to their speculative patter, one to the other.

"Twin-engine machine at three o'clock, Blondie," Clin passed the information to his Mid-upper. There was a short pause as all seven of us sweated out the possibilities.

"Got him," returned Ivor, his voice low, a mixture of apprehension and satisfaction.

Free of bombs, I braced for a possible corkscrew, but still held steady.

"I've got him in the gun sight," Clin announced.

"So have I," Blondie assured. We could all feel the tension building up.

"You ready to go?" Clin asked. Jack, too, was now behind the guns in the front turret.

"Whoops!" I think this was Ivor.

"What happened?" I yelled.

"It shot off like greased lightning!" Clin sounded relieved. "I'm sure it was a Messerschmitt 110."

As our adrenalin eased back a little, I uttered the now familiar message: "Shady side of the target. Watch your backs." My windscreen was beginning to freeze

217

over, and the de-icing jet wasn't up to the job. So far, more than half of the screen was still free, so there was no great urgency.

"I haven't mentioned it up to now, Phil." Frank was looking none too happy.

"Why have I this sinking feeling that I'm not going to like this," I wedged in.

"There is an appreciable loss from number two port fuel tank," the Engineer informed, "and it's bad."

"How bad?" I asked. "And is there a chance of fire?"

"Well, yes, there's always the danger of fire with leaking fuel, but, providing we don't have to mess aro . . ."

"There's a hang-up, Phil," Jack interrupted, "and it's fused and live."

"Send me home." I was running short of come-back. "What the hell can possibly go wrong next?"

"It's got to go, Phil." Jack was adamant. "Come hell or high water."

"OK, Jack," I answered, aware that there was only one reply possible. "We'll dump it in one of the allotted spaces in the North Sea."

"Fair enough."

Time hadn't allowed it, but if we had found it quicker, we could have given it to the enemy.

However, Frank's petrol problem was still with us, and I could see he was waiting for an answer. What he had been about to say was, "providing we don't have to mess around". With a stubborn bomb on board, we would have to mess around.

"Do we have any slack at all, Frank?" I asked.

"Here's the situation," Frank explained. "There appears to be a broken fuel line at number two tank, port side. All of the other five tanks are intact. However, to get the 'gas' from number three to number one, I have to go through two. Yes, some of the petrol will get through, but some will also be lost in the transfer."

"In short?" I had to ask.

"It'll be tight," Frank finalised. "By the way, Skip," he added, "how's your windscreen? This one of mine is nearly frozen over."

"Ten minutes ago, Frank," I tried a mini-smile, "the ice on my windscreen was a big deal. You've just relegated it to the second division. Can I have a course for the North Sea, Gerry? We've got to get rid of a reluctant 500-pound bomb."

"Steer 295, Skip."

"295 it is."

An hour later the battle was on to ditch the 500-pounder, and battle it was. The little sod just wouldn't let go.

"They must have glued it in, Jack." I wasn't even trying to joke. "Any other time this would be fun, but, as you heard, we're rapidly running short of petrol."

"I know, Phil," Jack said sympathetically, "but try a vigorous dive and jerk up one more time. I'll work the jettison bar at the same time."

That did it. We lost the bomb.

"Steer 212, Skip,"

"Steering 212."

Time and time again I marvelled at the icy, calm efficiency of our Navigator. He must have saved our necks several times.

Now it was do-something-about-the-ice time. Getting little help from the de-icing fluid, there was only one way to go. I had to open the side clear-vision panel and, carefully and painstakingly, edge my gloved hand out to rub the ice off the perspex windscreen. At cruising speed, this was a risky exercise. If any air pressure got in between hand and perspex, it would whip the hand back, breaking what it could in the process. In the circuit, later, I would have to go through this procedure again.

"How's the 'gas', Frank?"

"It's low, Skip." There was a pause. "I mean, it's really low!"

I could only nod bleakly at the truth.

"Wish I could see clearly where I was going," was my moan.

Uncle was now on the downwind leg in the circuit, its front screens only partially clear of ice. Even as far as the crosswind leg, this mattered not. However, on the final approach, it really did matter.

"Jeez, Frank," I was struggling, "this is dangerous. I think I'm too high, and we're going too fast."

"Well, for frig's sake, Skip," Frank said earnestly, "don't go around again if you can possibly help it. I don't think we'd make it."

Still too fast, and with a couple of bumps, we were on the concrete.

"Bloody brake pressure's fading and here comes the end of the runway — with the bomb dump just beyond!"

As the concrete faded, I pulled Uncle around the corner and along the perimeter track, still going too fast.

"Did you see any other bomber go down?"

The interrogation had to be gone through, question by question, before we could get anywhere near that lovely crisp bacon, eggs, toast and golden-brown fried potatoes.

"What was the flak like?"

"Did you see any night fighters. Theirs or ours?"

"Did you see the effect on the target?"

"Any of the crew injured?"

And so on, and so on.

We had all chipped in with answers here and there, but the Intelligence Officer was now looking me straight in the eye.

"Well," he summed up, "this was more or less a routine operation for you?"

There was a pause to let wide eyes narrow down a bit.

"I suppose you could call it that," I acknowledged.

"With a little engine annoyance," Frank rounded off.

It was just as well there was no one around to get U-Uncle's side of the story.

CHAPTER
TEN

Friday The Thirteenth

"You're a cheerful bugger, Skip," quipped Clin. "This Op seems to have you nobbled. What are you worried about? When you've seen one Battle Order, you've seen them all."

"Maybe so," I persisted, "but try a little mathematics this time. We've carried out twelve operational safaris, right? Think about that one."

They thought about it. I've an idea Jack knew exactly what I was aiming at, but he said nothing. When the penny dropped for Blondie, he let the world know.

"Frig me, if there's a Battle Order on the board for tomorrow, we've hit the jackpot."

"Right on the button, Ivor," I agreed. "Tomorrow is Friday, and it's the 13th, *and*, the next operation we do will be our 13th."

That zonked the happy tittle-tattle for a bit.

"Cheer up," said Gerry to no one in particular. "We've already had two days free of Ops; tomorrow could be another blank."

It could be, but it wasn't. When we got back to Stradishall, there was a Battle Order on every noticeboard, and our names were right there, third

222

place from the top. We were in business. The times for the briefings rubbed salt into the wound. It was to be another night operation.

"Your target for tonight, gentlemen, is the port of Kiel yet again. We're hoping to continue the damage to warships and submarines in the harbours, and rattle up shore installations at the same time. Good luck!"

186 Squadron had carried out one or two night raids while we had been in residence, but so far we had been nobbled twice only. The system was finally catching up with us. Squadron Leader Bass had some pointers for the pilots.

"Timing at night, gentlemen, is vital. During daylight you should see when you are about to drop your bombs onto a friendly bomber, and likewise you should see when someone is about to drop their trouble on your head. That's not so easy to do in the dark. It's imperative we all keep exactly to our times to ensure we survive."

"The searchlights will be a new experience for some of you. Look out for the single blue beam drifting casually along the fringe of the action. That's the master beam. As it lingers out there, it is also lining up on some poor sod. Then, when he least expects it, wham, it's in like a shot, locking on to the plane of its choice, dragging twenty to thirty of the regular searchlights along with it. Enemy night fighters? Oh yes, they'll be there as usual, and there is really only one answer to that one. Keep looking! Keep looking! And keep looking! Any questions?"

There was something dramatic, almost mystical about that taxi run to the threshold of the runway. One by one, in the gathering dusk, the Lancasters wheeled majestically out of their protected parking areas and looped into the long line of bombers advancing in slowtime toward the take-off point. The plane at the head of the queue moved into place on the concrete in answer to the first green light from the caravan, starting its ever accelerating take-off run when given the second green. For the next few minutes it was breath-holding time. If an engine faltered now while we were astride 12,000 pounds of dynamite and toting full tanks of petrol, the locals would have the thrill of a lifetime. After one such explosion, so I was told, a machine gun from the bomber had been found in a wheat field over a mile from the runway.

There was no old-fashioned take-off this time, or fancy footwork of any kind. The patter was strictly according to the book, Frank repeating everything I requested as he carried out the action.

"Throttles up to the gate."

"Throttles up to the gate."

"Wheels up."

"Wheels up."

So the prescribed rote went on. Bring up five degrees of flap. Another five degrees of flap. All flap up . . .

"I'll wheel it around the field once, Gerry, and you can then give me the first course to steer as we come back over base."

"Right you are, Skip."

Another night attack on the Third Reich was under way. There were 650 bombers taking part this time, and yet, but for a few sightings over the actual target, we would see very little of one another. I took an instant liking to these night operations. The darkness gave the luxurious feeling of security, allowing us to melt into the gloom, apparently safe from enemy fighters. This was false presumption, of course.

In the dark, the chance of collision with one of our own bombers was very real, especially over or near the target. Indeed, as we were to find out, a collision could occur almost anywhere along a night run. True, the darkness offered cover of a kind, but then it provided exactly the same service for the enemy. Their night fighters could infiltrate the bomber stream undetected, something they could never do in daylight. While we had our own very visual fighter cover during the day, any night cover was out of sight. And, darkness or not, there was no place to hide from the radar beams. As with their friends directing the anti-aircraft guns down at ground level, the enemy night fighters had their radar beams hooked up to their guns.

With the aid of ground-based radar, the night fighters could be vectored on to the incoming armada of Allied heavy bombers. But, thought these ingenious German innovators, why was it necessary to mix in with the actual bomber stream to shoot them out of the sky? Why not fly, say, above, below, or at the side of the stream — indeed at any angle at all — and fire from there? So the twin-engine enemy night fighters arrived on the scene with guns poking out from all sorts of unexpected places. The guns could be half-way back in the fuselage of the fighter and pointing upwards, downwards, or sideways. Just as long as the radar beam was pointing in the same direction as the guns, there was no problem. The pilot simply monitored his radar equipment, aligned his flight path to coincide with that of the bomber stream, and waited for a bomber to present a full image. When it did, the pilot would press the firing button and blow the bomber out of contention, making sure his own fighter was well clear of any possible explosion.

We were now super sensitive to all vague images lurking out there in the gloom. It was a sensitivity that fostered dangers of its own, and these had nothing to do with cannon shells.

There was something cosy about the dark, encouraging the ridiculous illusion that we were the only plane around. Fifteen minutes before the target, the illusion became less firm. Other four-engine silhouettes began to drift across the glare of the attack. The importance of timing also began to make sense. The planners, at briefing time, had built in safety precautions to try to avert collisions.

The stream undulates through the night sky like an apparently endless monster. Heights for each bomber varied from 18,000 feet to 18,500 feet to 19,000, and so on all the way up to 21,000 feet, and then all the way down again to 18,000 feet in the same 500-foot differentials. This pattern, going up and down, was in vogue from the vanguard of the attack to the rearguard of any bomber stream, by day or by night. Success, most especially in the dark, depended on that all-important timing factor. With a little out-of-sequence variation in flying times or wind factors, the picture could change dramatically.

Bombers on a required 18,000-foot level could drift forward or backward below the bombs of the planes above. Similarly, those on a required 21,000-foot level could drive forward or back above the planes below. There is little doubt that this drifting was responsible for bombers bombing other bombers, accounting for quite a number of our planes disappearing without trace over a target, their destruction then accredited quite erroneously to the accuracy of enemy flak.

As we closed in relentlessly on our second night target with its mayhem and menace, we realised yet again that this was a whole new way of going to war.

Flak, the number one terror merchant during the day, was greatly subdued by night. Only the exploding anti-aircraft shells were visible now and, mercifully, those hundreds of hideous pock puffs of spent flak could no longer be seen. "Spoofs" too, had lost a lot of their psychological impact under cover of darkness. This was all good news for what it was worth. The visual terror of the flak had been muffled, but its capability to knock us out of the sky was as potent as ever. Then there was the bad news.

As a menace, both visual and actual, the searchlights now replaced the flak. Their ceaseless arcing and probing beams on the run-in to the target created the impression of flying into a field of very tall illuminated grass. As we started our initial approach over Kiel harbour, things were really bubbling and boiling along, the noise building up all the while. I was just about to reiterate the old warning to the gunners to keep searching the gloom, when Gerry cut me out.

"Sorry, Phil, there's a tail wind. We're too early."

"Ah yes. Any ideas?"

"How about a dog-leg?" suggested the Navigator.

"Going into a dog-leg right now to port," I assured our Navigator, sounding a hell of a lot more confident than I felt. I wheeled the Lancaster over to the side about 45 degrees, and held this course as it took us away from the stream. After about a minute of this, I turned around 180 degrees to complete the circle, and we angled in to join the stream all over again. It was a dicey business for several reasons.

Rejoining the stream, we had to be careful not to whack into another bomber, to say nothing of the easy target we must have made for both the night fighters and the flak as we singled ourselves out from the stream. As it was, a collision very nearly did come off.

I didn't notice the other Lancaster about 500 feet above us, but luckily Blondie did. Apparently its pilot, quite understandably feeling twitchy anyway at this delicate time in his life cycle, mistook me for a night fighter coming in from the side for an attack. He went churning into a full corkscrew manoeuvre in self-defence.

"Dive, Skip," yelled Blondie. "Fast!"

I did a rapid dive to the left, the thought of our bomb load hovering vaguely at the back of my mind. The other thought was collision, brought about by evading one bomber and diving smack into another. "Peter" levelled off gently, and we started in on the run again. This, I thought, is living life really dangerously. To accommodate the all-important time factor, there we were poncing around this lethal piece of airspace like kids out for a joyride.

"That's the second time, Blondie," I reminded our Mid-upper, "that you've saved us from being crushed from above."

"Plane behind us been hit by flak, Skip."

This came from Clin in the rear turret, and I was intrigued by the matter-of-fact tone he had used. Better watch out, I thought, or we're in danger of becoming too familiar with this business of riding along the edge of doom.

"Anything else to see, Clin?"

"Nope."

Just as the boss had warned, there they were. Sinister blue master searchlight beams were ranging along the fringes of the target, their casual meandering appearing almost friendly. Suddenly, lightning fast, one of the blue beams locked on to a plane, bringing other beams along with it. Once coned — caught at the tip of a cone of twenty to thirty beams — the plane found it the very dickens to shake them off. The ack-ack batteries then gave this visual target their undivided attention, and other bombers in the stream avoided their luckless colleague like the plague!

"Bomb doors open."

Now we could get down to the main event of the evening.

The harbour installations were well alight. We could see the 4,000-pound blockbusters erupting all over the place. It was hell up here, but it must have been double hell down there. We had just about finished that nerve-racking thirty-second photographic run when the order to dive came again. Clin was the spur this time.

"Get down, Skip!" he ordered urgently. "There's a bloody bomber settling in on top of us."

This time I could afford to drop the stick more sharply, ducking out of trouble one more time.

"Jesus Christ," said Ivor, the tone a cross between rage and shock, "we're in more danger from our own friggin' bombers than we are from the bloody Krauts."

The Mid-upper had a point.

"Watch your backs everybody," I suggested as we eased away from the holocaust that was Kiel. "This is fun time for the night fighters."

At night it was all danger time. Over the target, there was the clamour, combat, and carnage that tended to weaken the cohesion of things quite a bit. Sneaking away from the place, we might delight in the sheer relief that we had squeezed through the mincer one more time, but this could create its own problems. Scrambling for the anonymity of the darkness, bubbling over with relief, crews seemed to overrate the cosiness of the gloom coming in all around them. It was by no means a sanctuary. The enemy fighters were aware of this relief factor, and were still very much in action at this vulnerable time of the attack. Wise bomber crews continued the vigilance, their probing eyes being rubber necked into every quadrant of the night sky.

Through the murk and scudding clouds, the faintest glimmer of a red- or white-hot exhaust anywhere within their airspace would make a crew nervous. Just as that bomber had corkscrewed near the target when we approached the stream from the side, so, too, were we ourselves about to be put on the rack.

Twenty minutes out of Kiel it appeared: a faint glimmer shimmering vaguely in the gloom about five to seven hundred feet above and behind us, maybe just a shade out to the starboard side. Something was marking time on us, its engine exhausts showing up in the dark. Clin saw it first and his news hustled all of our instincts back on to a razor's edge. Almost in reflex action, each member of the crew braced and readied himself, the old survival wariness sharpening up.

Rear Gunner, Mid-upper Gunner, and the Air Bomber slipped the safety catches off their gun clusters. The Navigator and the Wireless Operator retrieved all loose pieces of equipment on their table tops. Frankie checked that the engines were hooked up to the fullest tanks, and then he, too, riveted his eyes on the mysterious, blurred sort of glow. I slipped the switch clear of the automatic pilot and took over manual control. Locked into a stand-off, all seven of us were waiting and worrying.

Just what the hell was that "thing" up there, holding the same course as our bomber, and poised ominously about 500 feet above us. One of ours? Maybe. One of theirs? Again, maybe. The tension was building.

Everyone knew what was coming next. If the tension broke, and our patience ran out of steam, then way along at the end of this stream of protective twitching there was one last measure of self-preservation open to us — the corkscrew.

"While we're messing around here, Skip," Frank suggested, "our fancy man up there could be lining us up for the hammer."

I agreed with our Engineer, nodded, and got set to go.

"Corkscrew, corkscrew, rolling over the edge, now . . . Down port . . . Rolling . . ."

The tension had cracked on the edge of Frankie's ominous suggestion, and I, at least, had enjoyed the corkscrewing. The mystery of the faint glare would remain a mystery. Was it an enemy fighter? Was it one of our own bombers? Did the corkscrewing save our bacon? All were questions that would never, ever, be answered. Maybe Jack struck the right note.

"This is tiring, and it's very dangerous."

Maybe so, but if we all thought the action was over for the night, we were very much mistaken.

Stradishall Control Tower now held us in its tender care. Despite the fact that we had seen very little of each other since take-off nearly six-and-a-half hours earlier, there we were, all hitting home base about the same time. Control had no alternative but to stack us up and filter us in turn, down through the holding heights onto the runway. This was a vital time to hang on to one more lesson.

In the subtle trick of staying alive, we knew there was nothing more dangerous than apathy, a feeling of relaxation easing in on the downhill ride brought on by sheer exhaustion. As many of the ghosts of our predecessors knew very well, the bomber's last mile home could be the most dangerous of all, especially after a night operation.

We were well aware of and fully respected the set-up booby trap the Luftwaffe had pulled time and again. The Drem airfield lighting system was now laid out at Stradishall for all to see. If there were any enemy night fighters around, they had but to click into the bomber stream and ride in with the happy, carefree, "almost home" aircrews.

Fritz would wait until he had one Lancaster slowing up on the runway, and another hanging by its eyelashes on the final approach, fully committed, flaps and undercarriage reducing it to a sitting duck. Then, bingo, the Messerschmitt 110 pilot would boom in, leaning heavily on the firing button as he did so, belting the bombers with everything he had.

We knew it was a fair cop whichever way we looked at it. After all, we had just finished spreading our filth all over his front lawn and so our Luftwaffe counterpart was merely levelling out the score. Such were the thoughts and knowledge that kept us on our toes on the night of 13 April, our Lancaster jockeying for a landing position. In Peter, every spare pair of eyes was probing the gloom in all directions.

Then it came . . .

Way over on our left, forward, and almost down at circuit height, there was one boomer of a flash and explosion.

"Those bastards have done it again," came the shocked reaction over the RT from our Mid-upper Gunner. "There must be a night fighter around here somewhere."

The lingering silence from the rest of us offered mute agreement. We were quite wrong. As we trooped in from the motor transport wagon, having made our own nerve-tingling filter-in approach and landing, we learned that the tragedy had been self-imposed. One pilot, possibly over-anxious for his steak and eggs, or maybe reduced to a state of couldn't-care-less by six-and-a-half hours of operational night flying, had decided to beat the system by taking a short cut. It was a short cut to Hell. His Lancaster ploughed into another and a full-blooded collision resulted.

Throughout the night and all of the following day, the clean-up continued. Ten bodies were found, and there were three survivors, ironically one of these being the pilot who had decided to cut the corner. One aircrew member, the fourteenth, seemed to have vanished completely.

By daylight all spare personnel, aircrew and ground crew alike, were linked arm-in-arm in one mighty line, and the countryside was combed in every direction. The result was a negative. The fourteenth flyer could not be found. Not, that is, until a week later. When the heavy equipment finally winched up the remains of one of the broken Lancasters, they discovered the missing body, hidden completely by one of the Rolls-Royce Merlin engines.

CHAPTER
ELEVEN

But Not For Me

"May I join the wake?"

I recognised the voice and was already switching on a smile as I swivelled around on the dining-room chair. Judy Melville was standing right behind the chair next to mine.

"Hello there," I managed to say, trying to get rid of the "frog" in my throat. A firm hand on my shoulder stopped me from getting to my feet.

With no one to talk to, I had been staring solemnly at the bottom of my empty soup plate, thoughts and speculations bouncing around all over the place. The thoughts, I assured Judy, were not as black as my look might have implied.

"It wasn't so much our present way of life that was occupying my idle thoughts; it was more speculation on what's coming up just around the corner. This war has about had its chips. No country, not even the mighty Third Reich, can go on taking the sort of pounding we're handing out these days."

"Maybe so," Judy continued, "but they're not lying down yet, are they? I've just been reading through the recent reports, including the debriefing statements from your safari to Kiel harbour the other night, and we've got to hand it to these Germans. They keep bouncing back."

With no wish to hang on to that topic, I switched the subject to the social scene.

"What say we do the movie at the station cinema, or are you booked for some overtime at the office?"

"The movie idea sounds fine to me," agreed Judy. "Meet you back here in five minutes."

There was something genuinely friendly and agreeable about this WAAF officer. She was easy to talk with, and had no pretensions or elevated awareness of her own run-away good looks. Better watch your back, chap, I thought, as Judy came rippling down the stairs and back along the corridor toward the foyer.

All casual and carefree, the pair of us saw one more station movie together before I plucked up enough courage to try something more ambitious. How about a meal and a show in Cambridge? Straight away, her face reflected all sorts of guards and hesitations.

"No fancy footwork." I smiled. "No ulterior motive. Strictly the meal and the show."

Judy visibly relaxed, returning the smile. We agreed to try the Cambridge visit on the following Wednesday, providing business didn't get in the way. Maybe it wouldn't be a bad idea if a little guard and hesitation fell into place around my shoulders, too. Judy had already made it clear that she had been hurt enough.

Her message was quite clear. Pilots, like giant pandas, were a brittle, endangered species, forever teetering along the edge of extinction. Better if she

236

could just like them, joke with them, have drinks with them, even go out on the town with them, but never, ever, fall in love with them.

Wednesday was hassle-free, and the Cambridge visit was on.

"You really do have fun, Philip, don't you, every time you go near Kiel? I've been reading through the debriefing notes for last night, your second visit to the port. It all sounded a bit hairy."

We had just left the cinema and were searching around for the unique: a hotel or restaurant that could transform the severe ration quotas of wartime into minor culinary miracles. It was one of the favourite pastimes of the day.

"Yes, hairy would be a fair description of last night's Kiel affair," I admitted, "our second go at the place, as you say."

"We lost Halford last night," Judy pointed out. "He was in O-Oboe."

"Yes, but I'd have to say that I hardly knew him. He was quite new, and it was only his third Op. The word around the flight seemed to suggest that his plane didn't get the chop over the target, so it must have been jumped by a fighter on the way home."

"Can I ask you something, Philip?" Judy said, almost apologetically.

"Sure, go ahead."

"What does it feel like?"

The question stopped me in my tracks. It was not the sort of query I had expected.

"You are talking about Ops, aren't you?" I thought I'd better make sure.

"Well, I wasn't talking about in bed," she said, laughing.

This girl didn't believe in mincing her words.

"Why don't you come along with us next time and find out?"

I may have thought my remark funny, but the lady didn't laugh.

"Stop fooling, Philip. I'm serious. What does it feel like?"

"You really are serious, aren't you? Tell you what, this hotel looks quite good. Let's take a chance, have a drink, and see if they can rustle up a meal. D'you agree?"

"This hotel looks just fine," Judy agreed, but I could see that she hadn't even looked at the place.

"You want to know what it feels like, and I'll do my best to put it in a nutshell. If you think it all comes out as the square-jawed hero stuff we see in the movies, then Lady, I have news for you."

Judy said not a word, sipped her drink, pulled her chair a bit closer, and just listened.

"At Stradishall we are usually daylighters, as you well know, and that means we have to fly into that sea of flak and ugly black puffs of smoke over the target. It's a terrifying sight, Judy; scares the pants off me. At night the black puffs disappear, and those blasted search-lights take their place. In that second night raid on Kiel, we were caught in a cone of them, dragged into it by one of those master blue lights. We didn't half weave and skid around to get out of the glare."

"Each member of the crew has his own personal fear and dislike. The Mid-upper Gunner admits that his greatest anxiety is the 'hit on the head' phobia, looking above his head and seeing several bombers hanging in the sky above us, bomb doors wide open, each one jockeying for position to drop its bombs. My own greatest problem is that of priorities. Over the target, the flying has to be accurate to help the Air Bomber. I have to pay attention to the instruments, while at the same time watching out for other bombers close by; watching out for fighters; listening to and acting on the instructions of the Air Bomber; listening to and acting on the instructions of the Navigator; taking any evasive action the gunners advise; and all the while monitoring the scene of confusion, destruction and carnage taking place right outside my own front window. Strangely, the destruction going on at ground level far below is of little interest. Survival and getting the job done take pride of place."

"There's one part of the story, though, you should know, Judy, and that's the bit that most narratives leave in the closet. It's the point in the saga where they let the horror of the cannon and anti-aircraft fire go echoing off into oblivion, and so bring the tale to a 'happy ever after' conclusion. Pity really, because the writers are eliminating all the human touches of realism, the bits where the mouth is so dry that it seems even our chewing gum has turned to sawdust; where sweat cascades down the small of the back, and bubbles

239

out of the palms of both hands; the bit where you can feel the contents of your bowels turning to water, and your stomach nerves are doing somersaults."

"Judy, let's be honest, this could be boring you into the ground."

My friend across the table said nothing, waved my remark aside impatiently, and signalled for me to carry on, settling back to listen anew.

"Well, Judy, there is not much more to tell. Though it would be a rather large mistake to forget about the really big one, our old 'friend', Fear. You'll find this is the factor most narrators and chroniclers omit because, well, it's bad for the image, isn't it? But it's there all right, sitting on every shoulder. How could it be otherwise, when you know there are a lot of skilled people out there trying very hard to kill you? I mean, they're really trying! All you have to do is look through the front window and see the savagery over the target, and some of your friends being cut down out of the stream as you watch. You can feel Fear rippling up from the nape of your neck to the top of your head, before dissipating all over the place. Believe me, between the carnage and the chaos out front, and the unknown plotting going on behind, this is one gig Fear wouldn't miss for the world. I'd say here would be a fair time to listen to the man and to the advice he has to offer: 'Never ask for whom the bell tolls!'"

I had a sip of my drink, and smiled at Judy.

"Just as I told you, nothing at all like Hollywood, was it?"

240

"Thank you," Judy said quite seriously, ignoring my flippant remark. "You've filled in a lot of the blanks for me."

"Let's go eat," I suggested.

"Let's."

CHAPTER
TWELVE

Gee-H Leader

"Let me see if I can guess, Skip." Gerry was sitting next to me in the transporter. "You were trying to figure out how a nice Scottish boy like you got mixed up in a ruthless business like this. Am I close?"

Aware of my silence and the sombre expression to match, our Navigator must have decided to break the spell.

"Then again, Gerry," I answered, replacing the sombre stare with a smile, "maybe I was trying to figure my way out of another problem. That's the one where I'm always surrounded by a bevy of six Englishmen."

Our transport was now on the move, wheeling us out to V-Victor, the Lancaster designated to carry us to our target for today: Bremen.

"Truth to tell," I continued, "I was thinking about the boss."

"You mean the WingCo?" the Navigator queried.

"No, no," I explained. "The big boss of the Command, 'Bomber' Harris. He enjoys the sort of loyalty from his aircrews which borders on the mystical. What I was trying to figure out was: Just how does he pull it off?"

242

Now Gerry had the frown.

"That's a tricky question, Skip," he had to concede, "because our number one is not the most popular commander with the rest of Britain's military élite."

"And that, my friend, could be part of the answer," I reasoned, watching the other crew on the transporter file off at the huge circular concrete pad housing their Lancaster. "'Bomber' Harris is waging war on the enemy his way: head on, no messing around, no quarter given and none expected. Our boss seems to have come to terms with the fact that this is an enemy who can be whacked one way only. We have to punch him right into the ground. Anything less and we'd find that a wounded Germany would be just like a wounded tiger: more ferocious and dangerous than before."

"And you reason," Gerry saw that we were approaching the parking circle of V-Victor, "that this is why our army and navy types, and even some of his own Royal Air Force colleagues, dislike the boss?"

"That, and the fact that he treats his aircrews like blood brothers. He protects and cossets them any way he can."

The transport pulled up, the seven of us piling out to meet our bomber for today. Victor was obviously revelling in all of the attention coming his way. Ground staff personnel had been fussing over engines and airframe; the "gas" crew had filled up all six wing tanks with over 2,000 gallons of petrol; armourers had hooked up 12,000 pounds of high explosives into the cradles in Victor's long 33-foot bomb bay; and now, right on schedule, seven more "hopefuls" had arrived on the scene to continue the fussing.

We had time on hand before start-up, time to dump our gear inside the Lancaster and fool around and joke in general with the ground crew.

I was the only one of the seven to have a "seat" parachute. This is a relatively heavy affair, permanently fixed to its straps and harness, one which fits neatly into the pilot's seat of any Service plane, from trainer to four-engine bomber.

On arrival at the parking pen, I invariably got rid of this weighty life-saver quickly, climbing up the ladder at the rear of the bomber, and forward to the pilot's armour-plated seat on the flight deck.

For me, the inside of a Lancaster had an aroma all of its own. There was a hint of oil, petrol, glycol, raw oxygen and — would you believe — excitement. No doubt that ingredient, Excitement, could be questioned, but it was there all right, holding hands with its cousins, Fear and Foreboding. Over enemy territory, and especially over the holocaust of a target itself, they were a presence you could not only smell, but both feel and taste.

That was the inside.

On the outside, Victor stood proud, fully armed, ready for battle.

"You know very well you can't do that to Der Führer, Ivor." I was watching our Mid-upper chalk one of his erotic suggestions across the side of the 4,000 pound blockbuster in the bomb bay. "It's illegal."

244

"It's also disgusting," added our Rear Gunner, about to scribble some message of his own on a 500-pounder, "but I like it."

Jack, ignoring the fatuous outpourings of the various authors-in-chalk, was inspecting the contents of the bomb bay from a professional point of view. Any flaws or kinks our Air Bomber could find now would be rectified. Once in the air, any grief showing up had to be dealt with by remote control. If it couldn't be rectified, then we would just have to live with it. There were more than enough problems to be dealt with in the middle of a set-to, without worrying unduly about a 500-pounder that had gone all shy on us, and was refusing to leave its cradle.

Jack noticed me looking quizzically along the thirty-three-foot length of Victor's bomb bay.

"Impressive sight, isn't it?" he suggested, joining me on the concrete. "One four thousand-pounder and sixteen five-hundreds."

"Yes, you're right," I had to agree. "It is impressive. Twelve thousand pounds of very legitimate payback. I'm ecstatic that we're on the delivery end, and not on the receiving end."

"Especially this time," added the Air Bomber.

"Why this time?" I asked, curious and not a little intrigued. "Surely when you've seen one bomb, you've seen them all."

Jack thought it time to enlighten the ill-informed.

"Our leaders must have been in a particularly vicious mood this time," our Air Bomber explained. "Two of these five hundreds are fitted with time-fuses, a favourite trick of the Luftwaffe itself. One has a 24-hour delay, while the second five hundred will lie possum for six days before it detonates."

"That," I had to admit, "is devious. Still, fair's fair. If they did it to us . . ."

"Don't let it concern you, Skip," Harry chipped in. "You know very well what those sods did to my home town."

Our radio man was a citizen of the Metropolis, London, and yes, I had seen the end results of enemy bombing of that city.

Still, there was more creative writing to be done. Without a trace of humility, I, too, started in on one of the bombs with my chalk stick, scribbling my inanities down one more time. My message announced the now routine "Gray always comes back"! Today, nearly a thousand years later, I still shudder at this blatant piece of youthful arrogance; the vanity of someone too young to realise that only a fool would try to nail Destiny to the barn door.

Twenty-five minutes later, Destiny would have her chance to even the score. Lancaster V-Victor, bomb doors now sealed, all four Merlin engines murmuring away sweetly, stood at the threshold of the runway-in-use. One vital flash of a green Aldis lamp had placed the bomber, together with the seven members of her crew, on the starting line. Flash number two, the big one, was like a starter's pistol. Once discharged, and the unstoppable was on the way downhill. All four engines were opened to zero boost against the brakes, a check was made to see that the response was even on all four units, throttles were then pulled right back, and there was a hairline pause in time. Amid the hissing fury of air brakes being relieved of their burden, I would start to advance all four throttles gently, firmly, inexorably, checking that delicate tendency to swing to port. Trick was to get the tail off the deck as quickly as practical, placing the bomber at a better flight angle.

The Flight Engineer followed my take-off advance of the throttles, his hand lingering just behind the four levers. When I let go of the throttles to use both hands to ease back the control column, and thereby lift the Lancaster off the runway, Frank would hold all four throttles at the take-off position, securing them against the danger of then falling back.

As it happened, none of this was to take place according to plan. Destiny was playing games elsewhere.

True, Frank and I were both on the same flight deck, but priority had our heads pointing in different directions. While the Engineer was monitoring the take-off run of P-Peter, the bomber immediately ahead of us, my eyes were focused firmly on the runway control caravan. With one green down, the next one would give the go-ahead for my all-or-nothing Geronimo down the concrete.

"One thing's for sure," the remark was Frank's, "you can't fault this business for lack of variety."

"What you got now, Frank?" I asked, my interest casual, bordering on the non-existent. The coming of that second green from the caravan was paramount. Everything else was trivia.

"P-Peter up front just burst a tyre."

That paramount, I had to admit, was more important than my paramount. The caravan thought so too, and blocked our take-off with a steady stay-where-you-are red.

"Those guys in Peter were lucky," Jack reckoned from the side aisle, "the tyre lost interest just as the plane eased off the deck."

"He must've been raking along around a hundred mph at the time." I was guessing, not daring to mention the alternative. Jack dared.

"If that tyre had burst just five seconds sooner," our Air Bomber reasoned, "that crew would have become instant local folklore."

"Looks like the whole bloody wheel came off," Frank updated us.

Sure enough, we had to continue to mark time at the starter's gate, while a ground crew hared down the runway in a pickup truck to retrieve Peter's wheel and shredded tyre.

"Once off the deck," Frank said trying to soften things down, "they'd never miss the wheel."

"You've got a point there," I agreed with the Engineer. "Then again, it could have come in bloody handy when they got ba . . . Whoops!"

I didn't get a chance to finish the "back home again" part of the sentence. A hurry-along green from the caravan cut through our nervous backchat, urging me to get on with my own death-or-glory swing down the runway.

186 Squadron was only one small segment of the three hundred and twenty bombers in this particular

stream. Nevertheless, our boss would be anxious to hold up his end, keeping faith with his masters.

Sooner or later though, ignoring the evil intentions of enemy fighters, anti-aircraft shells, and other assorted hazards, the pilot of Peter would have to put that bomber back on the deck again. With only one good wheel at his disposal, the landing would have to be carried out with the plane's undercarriage fully retracted.

"Some people have all the fun." I had let the thought escape as the spoken word.

"What was that, Skip?" The Flight Engineer was right alongside.

"Nothing, Frank," I killed the thought. "It wasn't important."

Bremen had all the qualifications that guaranteed the city a permanent place near the top of Bomber Command's "hit" list. Together with Bremerhaven as its sea link, Bremen ranked second in importance only to Hamburg as a port. Then, as we were told at briefing, there are extensive railway marshalling yards, chemical industries, and — possibly the most important attraction — shipbuilding.

To add to V-Victor's vanity, our bomber was riding along in the number one position, our crew having been given pride of place. We were a Gee-H leader and at the head of the Squadron. Our Lancaster was at the front of four V-formations of three planes each: twelve bombers in all.

However, as Bremen was about to make clear, vanity or pride of place counted for nothing in the city's current back-to-the-wall situation. Protectors of the place were well aware that the Allied armies were right at the front door, a fact that seemed to inspire them to cling to one of my father's prime pieces of advice: If you have to go down, then make sure that you go down in style.

Enemy flak kept pumping up at us during the whole of what was to become one of the longest bombing runs we had ever made, the affair dragging on for close to twenty-five minutes.

"You have to give these bastards full marks for sheer tenacity," conceded Ivor from the mid-upper turret. "They know they're whacked, but they just won't lie down."

This attack on Bremen had been designated as a ground-support target, a fact which called for a high measure of accuracy. Our own ground troops were close by, and no doubt reconnaissance units would already be probing into the city suburbs. If we had spread any of our trouble outside the aim point, we could have ended up bombing our own people.

"Everyone still alive?"

I asked the question as we cleared the far side of the target. Five affirmatives out of six came back. Harry, the missing sixth call, was hooked into base with his radio, giving the thumbs-up when tapped on the shoulder.

"How about you, Skip?" Frank was looking in my direction. "You've still got three hours' flying to hack through."

"The flying's fine, Frank," I assured our Engineer, "but I've got to brace myself every time for the horror of that target run. We've all grown accustomed to the routine dangers but, like the rest of you, I'm aware that the unexpected can happen at any time and blow our world apart."

Frank nodded his understanding.

The formations broke up at five degrees east, leaving each crew to find its own way back to base. Victor had flown into some beautiful weather, blue skies above and bulbous, friendly cumulus clouds decorating everything below up to ten thousand feet. As we lost height very, very gradually, I could see the shadow of our bomber meandering carelessly through the picturesque canyons of pure white water vapour, leaping over one of the larger cumulus clouds from time to time. The scene was truly enchanting, the antithesis of the horror we had just left behind. Such beauty, plus the fact that "George", the automatic pilot, was now flying the plane, was dangerous. It encouraged lethargy, and that could kill.

"Watch your backs, everyone," I suggested. "We're not home yet."

Two hours later, on the downwind leg of the circuit, the familiar patter between the Pilot and the Engineer got under way. For every action I requested, there was a repetitive assurance from Frank as he carried out the manoeuvre.

"Undercarriage down."

"Undercarriage going down."

As the Engineer pushed the lever forward, we both checked visually and by ear. If any one of the four lights showed red, or the horn was activated, the landing

251

would be abandoned. There would be a flaw in the system somewhere.

"Pitch fully fine."

"Pitch fine."

The Engineer had set the propeller pitch at 3,000 revs per minute for each propeller.

"Fuel."

"Fuel booster pumps on."

"Flaps, twenty degrees."

"Flaps twenty."

As we clambered aboard the transporter taking us back to the interrogation room, I looked back at our Lancaster, V-Victor. I had forgotten to pat the pilot's seat and say the words before I left the flight deck, so I said them now.

"Thank you, my Friend."

CHAPTER
THIRTEEN

The Last Mile Home

There was no doubt about it. By late April 1945, World War Two was running out of steam. The shooting war was nearly over. As we were about to find out, though, this was one enemy who didn't back away easily. For our part, and although the boys and I didn't realise it at the time, this next flight over the Third Reich would be our last chance to play with real guns and real bombs. Operation number sixteen would bring our combat operations to a close.

"We're getting a great day for it, Skip." Harry was as bright as the morning itself.

"Bugger off, Jenkinson," growled Blondie, never at his best first thing in the morning. "We're about to dice with friggin' death, not jump into bed with someone, so try not to be so bloody cheerful about it."

"Piss off," Harry retorted, refusing to be put down. "We're a long time dead."

Gerry and I exchanged smiles. We weren't quite sure how to take the "long time dead" angle, but we were quite accustomed to the verbal crossfire. Just like the rest of us, Harry and Ivor got on very well together, but they didn't always reach their happy peak at the same time. Jack, forever the peacemaker, cut in quickly with a change of subject.

"Did we all read the papers this morning?" he wanted to know, glancing around. "They reckon we managed to sink the pocket battleship, *Admiral Scheer*, on that last crack we had at Kiel."

"Yes, I saw that," said Frank, "but did you have a look at those reconnaissance photographs? Beautiful! They show some of the docks at Kiel empty of water, and two-man miniature submarines decorating the place like dead beetles."

"D'you ever find out about those sand-bags, Phil?"

Gerry cut in with the question, and I could see by the reactions that everyone was interested. Twice this week, on non-operational days, we had been ordered into the sky with a load of sand-bags. These had been strapped up into the cradles in the bomb bay used by the 500-pound bombs, allowing Jack to make many runs over the bombing ranges by selecting one or two bags to drop each time. As pilot, I was ordered to get right down to deck level; to fly as low as I dared over the drop point. I'm sure we all enjoyed the whole affair.

"We could be dropping food parcels to people on the other side of the Channel. Whether it will be before or after the shooting war ends is not quite clear. I'm sure there's a definite tie-in between those panniers I saw in the Stores Section, and the sand-bag dropping."

There was silence while everyone thought this one through. Maybe I had better throw in the extra piece of gen I'd picked up from Judy.

254

"My special intelligence angle is pretty sure the drops will be made to the Dutch."

"Ah ha," came back Harry quick as a flash, eyes twinkling, "so it does pay to have friends in the right places. What we have to ask ourselves here is, in what sort of places and circumstances do we get this kind of information?"

There were knowing smiles all around.

"I think someone is trying to suggest, Phil, that maybe bed is the best place to get this sort of inside intelligence, bouncing off the pillow maybe," Frank hinted.

"Oh, I know what our wireless operator has in mind, Frank," I threw in my smile to join the others, "and I can assure you, a chance would be a good thing."

About here we found ourselves fronting up to the Briefing Room door, and the ribbing had to stop. On the other side of this particular entrance way, laughing and joking were out of style. The countdown for our operation number sixteen got under way.

"The target for today, gentlemen, is a little town in north Germany called Bad Oldesloe. It's situated between Bremen and Hamburg, and has a main railway line running through the town centre, linking to an important marshalling yard complex."

Judy Melville gave us her intelligence report, passing along words of warning as she delivered her message.

"We know for a fact that our own ground troops are all around this area, so we would ask you to exercise great care and accuracy with your bombing. It's a delicate situation. Then there is the matter of flak. Many of the enemy anti-aircraft guns are mobile, meaning that, as we push them back on the ground into a smaller and smaller area, so, too, do they pull back and concentrate more and more artillery into this smaller area. The flak could be heavy. Watch out!"

Clin, our Rear Gunner, had been admitted to the station hospital with a throat infection some days ago. We had been graced with a distinguished replacement in the rear turret. Flight Lieutenant Buckland, the gunnery leader for the Squadron, was our stand-in gunner.

The wagon wheeling us out to the dispersals came to a limping stop, and the glass panel at the rear of the driver's compartment was pushed to the open position. The WAAF driver peered back at us, all anxious and concerned.

"We've got a flat tyre." She confirmed what we had already suspected. "I could change it, of course, but you don't have that kind of time. Transport already know. I've called them on the RT. Trouble is, this is the last run, and the other two drivers may have gone."

We were approximately half a kilometre from R-Roger's dispersal so there was not much we could do about it. We certainly couldn't carry all of our gear and parachutes the remainder of the distance. The spare transport wagon eventually arrived. Now we were slipping back on the time schedule. Not too important except for one minor detail. We were set to fly right-hand plane to the WingCo in his V-formation, and it would not create a good impression if we arrived late.

If we skipped the capering around with the ground crew, and the chalking of our nonsensical messages on the bomb casings, we would be more or less on time. But then . . .

"The batteries on the starter trolley have gone flat." Frank looked at me mournfully as he passed on the bad news, his expression mirroring his disbelief. "The ground crew have signalled that they'll pick up a spare from the next pan."

We had been able to start up the port inner engine only, the other three sets of propellers hanging out there stationary and silent. A little bit of concern was beginning to creep into the cabin, caused mainly by what we could see happening at other dispersal points. All the Lancasters had four engines purring away happily. Finally, we too reached this welcome state, but there were still more wrinkles.

As Frank and I raced through the internal checks, we got as far as the run-up for the engines.

"You're not going to believe this, Frank." I had to share this black news with someone, and who better than the Engineer. "We're dropping two hundred revs on the port outer."

"Oh no!" Frank was getting mad. "Christ, what do these guys think we're on here, a cross-country exercise? Try blasting it a bit more, Phil."

The maximum drop we were allowed was 150 revs, and even that was too close. Now we were really beginning to fall behind. Some of the other Lancasters were already on the perimeter track, rumbling majestically toward the take-off point. I gave the nervous engine one long blast at full power, anchored it back, and then slowly eased it forward to 1,700 revs.

257

Both magnetos were tested again, the needle holding this time, mercifully, on the right side of 150.

"That's close enough, Skip." Frank was curt. "Let's get out of here."

I didn't let anyone know about it yet, but one more problem had crept in. For some obscure reason, our faithful Roger was not holding its brake pressure too well. This was a problem, yes, but not a world shaker. By the time we returned from the target the bombs would be gone so, what the hell. If we ran off the other end of the runway, it would save the farmer the job of ploughing his field. All I would have to do was taxi slowly, and stay well back from the loaded bomber in front of us. I would have lost Brownie points if I'd hit him, to say nothing of upsetting his rear gunner no end. Now to find the boss, hacking around up there waiting patiently for the starboard side of his formation.

The Wing Commander must have watched the Americans packing their planes into 36-ship formations, because he was getting very keen on tightening up our formation work. There were twelve Lancasters from 186 Squadron in this attack. The boss wanted us in four neat V-Vic formations of three, with R-Roger flying on his starboard side. "Get in close enough to see the worried look on the lead pilot's face," he had told us at briefing. I would have to work really hard at this hand-holding business all the way to the target and most of the way back. Happy days!

At least there was a bonus for Gerry this time. The lead navigator would take most of the responsibility, making sure we stayed at the correct height, and in the proper time slot. If he allowed his Lancaster to fall out of its scheduled place in the stream, then the whole Squadron would follow his mislead, and we all knew what that would mean. A bomber out of sequence in the stream was a menace to itself and all the other planes around it.

Closing in on the target, we began to appreciate Judy's reference to the flak. The city defences had guns everywhere and some to spare. There was a heavy concentration of anti-aircraft fire during the whole of the twenty-minute run up to and through the target. By the time we started the vital and final two-to-three-minute precision bomb run, the ack-ack shells were exploding on either side of us, below, above, in front, behind.

"Christ almighty," came the bewildered observation from the mid-upper turret, "these buggers are really out to get us, aren't they? You would think they were trying to kill us."

Nobody dared quip back, mostly, I'd guess, because they were thinking the same as I was: If the maidens down there can keep up this concentration of fire, they will indeed kill us all. Spoofs, too, were blasting off at regular intervals, even the medium flak giving us a hard time. In the middle of the bedlam, it was always wise to keep an eye on the medium stuff. These guns used smaller calibre shells, but they could pump up their goodies in greater numbers. The trick was to watch their arc of fire.

Like the bullets carried in the belts of our own turrets, the ammunition used by the lighter AA guns was served up to a set pattern: armour piercing, incendiary, anti-personnel, and other undesirables. We could see them curving away from the ground in an assortment of colours, presenting quite a beautiful picture. But the arc was the thing.

As long as we could see these smaller shells curling and bending in one direction or another, then they were curling and bending away from the bomber. It was danger time when they appeared to be stationary. This meant the pretty shells were coming straight for the bomber, a realisation that could trigger all sorts of reactions.

One of the Lancasters in our bevy of twelve bombers must have developed a nervous twitch while watching our fascinating coloured friends, because it suddenly writhed into evasive action, banked away sharply and lost its formation. Maybe I should have joined him. About ten to twelve seconds later, several blasts and explosions came uncomfortably close to the eleven of us still with the formation. Our lead plane shuddered visibly, while we ourselves got rocked around for a second or two.

"Have a look back there, Frank," I shouted above the noise, and between the instructions coming from the Air Bomber. "See if we've been dented anywhere."

Frankie gave the thumbs-up and disappeared back into the innards of the Lancaster. Harry got in his piece before Frank had returned from his inspection.

"Some of the RT and all of my WT aerials are knackered, Skip," he reported, "but there's no other damage around me as far as I can see."

When Frank got back he confirmed this good news. No holes, no fires, no scars to report. By now we had all decided to live dangerously. The bombers in our formation group had opened their bomb doors. With all of this shrapnel zipping aimlessly around our immediate air space, now we could break into a cold sweat. We were at the mercy of this curving, slicing, unpredictable flak.

Both in front and behind, the boys reported bombers swerving and diving to avoid exploding shells. There was thick cloud cover around ten thousand feet, but with radar being used by friend and enemy alike, the cloud could be ignored.

"One of these poor sods behind us must have been caught with its load still on board," the Bombing Leader told us from the rear turret, "because it went up like a Roman candle. One minute it was there, and the next it was spread all over the sky."

"There's a helluva lot of flak around," Blondie assured us, again from the mid-upper turret, not telling us anything new. It was as bad as we had ever experienced.

"Oil pressure is low on the port outer, Skip." Frank was merely informing me. He knew very well I could do nothing about it while we were hanging over the target.

"Bombs away."

"Thank Christ for that," cut in an obviously relieved Blondie.

Frank and I managed a sickly smile, one to the other. That was the first time Ivor had thanked anyone for

261

losing our bombs. The flak must have been niggling him.

"Keep a sharp lookout on this side of the target," I suggested to anyone who could hear me and was in a position to help. "These bloody fighters know very well we're as relieved as hell to get away from these frigging guns, and are liable to get careless. Don't give them a free go. If I have to, formation or not, WingCo or not, I'll corkscrew. Stuff the boss and his formation. Our survival comes first."

"With all that crap and corruption we've just dropped," a curious Jack wanted to know, "I wonder if we managed to hit any railway lines or rolling stock down there?" He was peering up at us from his glass-floored compartment at the front of the aircraft.

"I don't know about hitting trains, Jack," I smiled back at him, "but if there's anything travelling along the rail tracks at this moment, I'd advise the driver to get out of his cabin right now and run like hell. In less than five minutes our fighter cover will be down there at deck level shooting the crap out of everything sitting on a railway line."

There was no great happiness about our course for the first leg to take us back home. Some gumball at Head Office had routed us south through the Ruhr, resulting in a steady stream of flak popping away at us for quite some time. Then came another piece of bad news from Jack.

"We've got a hang-up, Phil," he yelled up to us. "One of the 500-pounders is still in the bomb bay, fused and ready to go."

"Now there's a thing," I answered, resorting to a piece of useless phraseology while I figured out what to do next. "Let's hang in with the formation for a bit, then we'll cut away and see if we can get shot of the sod."

This was when the oil pressure/brake pressure problem resurfaced. Hell! If we couldn't ditch that bloody bomb, there was every chance I'd have to put Roger down on the deck with fading brake pressure and a live ding-dong stuck under our feet. Now there was a thought to keep the pulses racing.

At six degrees east we cut away from the boss's formation and headed toward the North Sea, seeking out an area just beyond The Wash.

"OK, Jack. Let's have a go," I suggested.

"Bomb doors open," ordered our Bomb Aimer.

"Bomb doors open."

There was silence for a bit, while Jack did whatever air bombers do to get rid of shy, unwanted bombs that refuse to leave home. Time dragged on. Then came the black news.

"Stupid thing won't go, Phil," was the word from down front, "but try this. I'll set it up again, and when I say 'Ready!', do some of the old dive and jerk routine. When the nose goes up in a hurry, that should give the little sod a shock."

"OK, we'll have a go."

There was a short pause.

"Now, Skip!"

"Right! Diving!"

We lost about 500 feet and then, zip, up came the nose in a hurry. The good news arrived as fast as the nose passed up through the horizon.

"Great stuff, Phil," came Jack's glad tidings. "The hang-up's gone. That's one bomb Bad Oldesloe missed, and the fish in the North Sea got instead."

Surprisingly, not one of our Squadron Lancasters was lost, but our next-door neighbour, Chedburgh, was not so lucky. There was a spiral of smoke coming up from a paddock about a half-mile short of their main runway. A Lancaster had crashed into a tree. Hit over the target, the bomber had been trying to carry out an overshoot on three engines. There were no survivors.

Back at base, with no RT to contact the tower, and aerials flapping in the breeze, we fired off greens for permission to land.

"Just for old times' sake," I said when it seemed like a good time to let the boys in on the secret of the low brake pressure, "brace yourselves for a sudden stop. Our brake pressure could be losing interest."

"Why don't we try one of the emergency airfields, Woodbridge or Manston?" suggested our stand-in rear gunner.

"I'm sure we'll make it OK," I said, crossing all the fingers I could spare.

The sun was edging towards the horizon on what had been a wonderful, sunny day. Lady Luck surely wouldn't ball things up now.

All anchors out, wheels down, full flap, throttles right back, Roger dragged itself over the final approach at the minimum flying speed permissible, touching down as near to the start of the runway as possible. With everyone tensed for the full drama, the brakes and their support hydraulic pressure worked like a dream. We came to a dead stop with half the runway still to go.

"I think you're a bit of a scare merchant, Skip," quipped Blondie.

What could I say?

It could be reasoned that we owed our survival to skill, thorough training, experience, or perhaps just plain knowing when to duck. That would be a load of waffle. We knew very well the credit lay with a friend who had hung in there with us right down the line. She was a beautiful lady called Luck! True, we never actually set eyes on this most constant of all our companions, but every time we left the deck she must have been riding in our pockets. How else could we have got away with it all?

How else could we have dodged away from the screwed-up takeoff, fully loaded with bombs; the heart-stopping scrape over that hangar; the day fighters and night fighters; the collisions, the bullets, the shells, the anti-aircraft holocaust, the explosions, the criss-cross seas of shrapnel, the bombs cascading down from above; the searchlights, the dodgy engines, the faulty brake pressure, the landing back at base fully loaded with bombs, some murderous weather conditions and icing?

How else could we have watched from our privileged front-row seats as all hell broke loose around us; other bombers were carved up in front of us, below us, above us and behind us; coking plants were reduced to rubble and blazing infernos 20,000 feet below our toes; other Lancasters were hit and left to limp off home; our Squadron machines smashed into each other on the circuit; and unbelievable scenes of carnage and confusion were taking place just outside our windows? How else?

And now, by May, 1945, our bombing campaign was over. The uncompromising, unrelenting work was at an end.

Throughout its years at war, Bomber Command had unloaded a million tons of explosives over the Third Reich, losing eight-and-a-half thousand bombers in the process. A staggering fifty thousand aircrew were killed during the non-stop campaign, meaning that the chance of completing an operational tour was somewhere in the region of one in three.

To the survivors coming out the other side of the meat grinder, it seemed incredible that the historical and vital phrases of their tenuous trade were now just obsolete idioms. Echoing off into the canyons of "once-upon-a-time" were such dramatic phrases as "Enemy coast ahead", "Flak up front", "Bombs away", and "Fighter, port quarter, 10 o'clock high", phrases that could strike fear into the hearts of even the hardest men in the business.

Looking back over their shoulders, aircrew members must have pondered the thought that so much of their country's time and money, so much of their own personal time and sweat, had gone into the learning and perfecting of such a highly skilled, dangerous, tenuous profession, a profession that was out of date almost before the first signature hit the peace treaty.

When I looked back over my own shoulder, I could not ignore the many faces, smiles and memories that kept jostling for attention. Most of the faces were smiling, as if they were aware of the problems they were causing. I could see: Gorman, Nobby Clark, Chamberlain, Cunningham and Ginger Lewis, all killed while training in Arizona; Jack Evans, my friend at Ludlow, later killed in action; Smudger Smith, the New Zealander who had taught me how to fly a Lancaster; Flight Sergeant Morris and his crew, who had arrived at 186 Squadron the same time we did, all killed on their second operational flight before we had a chance to get to know them; Phil Garland, my friend at Carlisle, who had taught me the art of spit and polish; Henderson, Cousins and Hayworth, who had shared the same taciturn primary instructor at Falcon Field, Mr Lockridge; Ian Cameron, Roberts, Tate, Hunt, James, Cowley, Burson, and at least two other Australian pilots whom I can't now name. All of these, and possibly others who have escaped my recall, had got the chop during my time with the Squadron, each one taking his crew of six along with him.

Memories, like their owners, will always have their favourites, and my recall was no exception. Two faces boomed out of the ruckus, like a pair of diamonds in a glass factory: Mr Lockridge (whose first name I never did learn) and Ginger Lewis — especially Ginger. I kept seeing his lopsided smile propped up in the bed opposite me in the living quarters at Falcon Field. Poor old Ginger, cut down at the fabulous age of twenty-one, his star snuffed out before he could get into the shooting war. We had to move on and leave our friend behind, resting for ever in some obscure cemetery plot in the Arizona desert.

Rest, though, was not what our leaders had in mind for us. The killing and demolition contract may have expired; now for the tidying-up jobs.

CHAPTER
FOURTEEN

Ghosts Of Targets Past

There, it was happening again. Just as soon as Judy Melville moved into the Mess lounge, straight away the sun seemed to be shining just that little bit brighter, the coffee tasted much better, and even the headlines in the newspapers were infinitely happier. To spread icing all over the cake, this very beautiful lady from the Intelligence Section was walking straight toward my chair.

"What makes you so happy, Philip?" she enquired. "You're smiling all over your face."

If you'd just watched what I've just watched, I thought, and if you'd just thought what I've just thought, you would be smiling too. My laugh was involuntary.

"As you walked toward me, Judy, I realised there was no way in the world you could lose. You look equally as beautiful coming forward as you do when you're walking away. Does that answer your question?"

"Flattery," she laughed as she flopped none too elegantly into the soft leather chair next to mine, her long legs stretched straight out in front of her, "will get you everywhere."

"What's the word?" I asked, my question merely teasing the situation along. "Have you any vital secrets to share with the peasants?"

Judy smiled the smile of the informed, obviously aware that she did, indeed, have some interesting information tucked away in that lovely head of hers.

"Oh yes," she assured with a tantalising, far-away expression, deliberately allowing her glance to drift toward the flower beds outside the window. "I did just discover a rather interesting piece of news."

That was it. Finish. Even the provocative smile lost its place while Judy sipped slowly on her cup of coffee. My patience held as long as it could, finally tripping over its own ego.

"Well?" I asked, the monosyllable bubbling and exploding out of my curiosity, fully aware I was being sucked in. Judy's laugh was equally provocative.

"I said there was this interesting piece of information," she said, intentionally spacing out the words. "I didn't say I was going to babble out all the Company's secrets."

"Go on!" I encouraged. "Be a little devil. Ignore the expense. Babble them out anyway."

That managed to squeeze out another infectious chuckle.

"All right," the lady relented. "Just this once you can have the inside information before it has been released to the Station in general."

Judy paused for effect.

"I've just been presented with three days' leave." Now she really did laugh, watching my expression match the realisation that her "secret" information was about as secret as the newspaper headlines. "Sorry about that," Judy continued, "but I really was so pleased to get that leave pass. It seemed a great chance to string out the good news. All that aside, though, I would have to admit the work over the past few months has been wearing me down."

"Don't be sorry about a thing," I assured her. "Seeing you laughing and happy has got to be good, no matter whose funny bone has to be banged to make it happen. Then again, I wouldn't want you to imagine that you were the only winner in the time-off game."

The implication sank in.

"You mean . . .?"

"Yep. The boys and I have just got ourselves the self-same deal: three days off duty, three days to take the place by storm, wherever that place may happen to be."

From there the smiles, laughter, and humour melted into general conversation. Obviously there had been a decision in high places to grant leave across a fair part of the board now that unconditional surrender seemed imminent. It could be looked upon as a sort of calm before a new type of storm. We were sure that peace would bring no rest at all for aircrew. For the moment, though, leave was leave, and what we did three days from now was of no concern. That was a lifetime away.

"Where will you spend your time?" Judy asked.

"London, I suppose. Two of our boys are from the Metropolis anyway, and it's not really worth my while jacking all the way up to Scotland. By the time I got there it would be time to start back."

"London . . . mmm? Now isn't that a coincidence," mused my companion. "That's my intended destination, too."

"Let me guess," I ventured, pretty sure I was about to state the obvious. "London is your home town?"

"Not really. I'm from Shrewsbury, but my sister and her husband have a flat down there. I'll be using that."

And that is about the point where this topic of conversation could have sailed off into the sunset. Not so. There was this one further dinger of a question about to come hurtling around the corner.

"Where will you be staying down there, Philip?"

The short and truthful answer to that one was easy.

"I haven't the slightest idea," I replied, "but I've learned never to underestimate the resourcefulness of this crew. Last time we were in the big city of London, five of us got stuck way out at Crayford in Kent, about twenty miles from the city centre. Hotel or hostel accommodation was impossible to find so, nothing daunted, we tried the local police station. Could they help? No problem, said the Sergeant, and all five of us spent the night in the holding cells for overnight prisoners. The law men even provided us with a great breakfast of bacon and eggs."

Judy was quite amused at the thought of us tangling with the Crayford "carabinieri", but she had a much more civilised suggestion to offer for this latest roll into the capital.

"If it links in with your plans, and you have no hang-ups about the idea, you, too, could stay at my sister's place."

The offer was truly unexpected, and the surprise of it all had me struggling for a comeback. In the past, the boys and I had played these romps into town in the same mould as Don Quixote, meandering down whichever byway the horse chose. The beautiful thought of instant accommodation was pure luxury.

"Such an invitation, Judy, is obviously very generous and I could rush in with a quick 'Yes' and 'Thank you' before you change your mind, but aren't we both forgetting something? If it's your sister's place, there is every chance she may not take too kindly to a stranger from a strange land crowding in on her privacy."

That was when the quiet lady from Intelligence dropped her own little blockbuster.

"Oh, we won't be crowding any part of Jacqui's life. She's in Nottingham for a month to be near Alan, her husband. He's stationed at RAF Syerston, with Transport Command."

Well now, as our American friends would have said, you can shoot me twice. I've heard it all. This rather shy, mild-mannered maiden was just bubbling over with surprises. Not only was she offering me the use of her sister's home during my forty-eight hours in London, but she had rattled the word "we" into the conversation without a second thought. "We won't be crowding Jacqui," she had assured me.

What more was there to say?

"I'd be honoured to share your accommodation, ma'am, only you'll have to let me hold up my side of the picture. I'll contract to feed us. A deal?"

"A deal."

I could have added that as long as I was tagging along with her, I'd have made do with the back seat of a Number 29 bus, but I decided to let that extravagance go by. After all, the war years had somehow changed most of the rules. The more conservative ideas that had been in vogue five years before had moved over, making way for the new take-it-as-it-comes radical order of things. We had learned to live in a hurry, fall in and out of love much faster, and through whimsical quirks of fate, could even die at high speed. In short, what would come to be considered promiscuous a decade later was more or less a necessity during the uncertain days of the holocaust. This, as the Führer had glibly explained, was war.

So the Clueless Crew, as we had dubbed ourselves, together with one very desirable intelligence officer, rolled into King's Cross railway station. Hopes were riding out of sight with not a thing to worry about for three days. The mysteries of the Metropolis pulsed all around us. For now, there was no tomorrow.

"This is a very beautiful flat, Judy. Your sister and her husband must be relieved that it has survived the onslaught of the Luftwaffe, the doodlebugs, and the V-2s."

We were somewhere in the Kensington area, but that was about as close as I could figure it. On the outside, my guide obviously knew exactly where she was going, so I didn't really pay a great deal of attention. On the inside, I was sure we would both find out for ourselves where we were going. To that I was paying a great deal of attention.

"In the hazy, lazy days of peace, your brother-in-law must spend his time in the city," I suggested.

"Yes," Judy yelled through from her bedroom, "Alan is in property. I've no idea which area, but he was booming along just fine before this wrangle fell in on everyone's head. D'you fancy a cup of tea?"

"Great idea."

I still felt as though I was walking over slippery, unsure ground, half expecting to fall flat on my face at any minute. After all, what exactly did we have here? Two relatively cautious, timid individuals, neither one quite sure how the other felt about either the in-house situation or each other. By now I was adept at playing things by ear, but this was outrageous.

"What fantasies do you see in there?"

Judy's question broke the spell. I had been staring all glassy-eyed into the centre of the blazing coal fire, my imagination losing itself in the pulsing, twinkling red canyons in the hearth.

"I was wallowing in a growing puddle of reality," I admitted to my companion. "I'm a bit slow, I know, but it's just beginning to dawn on me, ever so gradually, that the boys and I have got away with it. We're free. We've actually gone through the very last of those operational mincers."

275

Now we were both staring at the magical, private visions and images being manufactured for us by the flames in the hot coal pieces.

"Yes, you're right, my lucky lad," Judy said, staring straight ahead. "It looks as though you'll be able to tell your grandchildren the story after all; the one where you shook hands with the devil, and lived to walk away.

"Sitting in front of the fire like this, all quiet and cosy, knowing that the killing has finally stopped, is like some impossible dream. For a while there I thought the massacre would never end. I found myself becoming almost paranoid standing up in front of the crews, time after time, many of the faces at the tables well known to me. The whole scenario was beginning to make me recoil in revulsion from the inevitable; the knowledge that the chance of all the faces coming back from an Op was nothing to minus z. In the bombers you were there, in the thick of it. You knew what was going on. Back at the airfield, all we could do was to wait, wonder, and worry."

Judy's words trailed off into silence. The warmth of the room all around us and the unfamiliar visions of a world at peace, quietly but persistently presented themselves for our cautious acceptance. Somehow the vision seemed alien: too much to expect.

"The idea takes a bit of getting used to, doesn't it?" Judy had turned her head in my direction, her expression questioning, uncertain, her hand inching along the settee in search of assurance.

I agreed, thinking back over all the weeks, months and years of work that had gone into my single-minded achievement, right up to where I had strapped myself into the seat of an operational Lancaster bomber.

"For the past four years, as my one and only youth slid down the tubes, I dreamed and scrambled and sweated to get into that bomber stream. Suddenly there is no more reason to scramble or sweat. The dream has run its course. It's over."

Almost involuntarily, my hand sought its own sanctuary. The hands found each other, held on tightly, and the tension of our mutual uncertainty started to melt away and roll downhill. Words, like the war itself, were no longer in fashion. The redundant Intelligence Officer and the no-longer-needed Bomber Pilot were suddenly holding on tightly to the one remaining constant in their thoughts — each other. The coming together was instinctive, its intensity a surprise to us both, but, once achieved, neither one was in any hurry to run for cover. As in the scene from *Lost Horizon*, we had found our own Shangri-La, however temporary it might prove to be. We had no intention of hurrying back into the blizzards and snow storms of the real world.

Lips and bodies were content to linger on in this soft and melt-away haven, indulging in each other's warmth and security. As we had collapsed in a heap on the settee, coming together like two magnets, Judy had somehow surfaced on top, and now lay astride the situation like a well put-together rag doll. Stresses and strains of the past months were fading and rippling away like unwanted echoes of a bad dream. For those beautiful, unhurried, careless moments, time lost interest and stood on its head.

Ever so gently, Judy feathered her lips away, prised herself up a little and, still with her eyes tightly closed, eased herself away onto the delicately patterned rug in front of the fireplace. Her robe seemed to sense that, at least for now, it was expendable. It fell away onto the carpet. As the trickle of traffic rolled by on the asphalt below, and the shadows on the walls danced to the whim of the flames in the hearth, we fused together once more. This time, ghosts of fear and tension and danger and confusion misted quietly back into the shadows in the corners of the room, their fading threats tip-toeing off into the obscurity of the night.

Two days later, Judy and I had exorcised a war.

CHAPTER
FIFTEEN

Let's Try The Peace Game

Happiness was in the air. Change and the early twinges of peace were everywhere. Just as Vera Lynn had promised, the lights were going on again all over the world.

Even our trusty old friends, the Lancasters, joined in the fun. On 8 May 1945, we were called early at 0215 hours. Our effort for Operation Manna was about to roll down the runway, this time our bombers transporting the necessities of life rather than the components of death and demolition.

The Allied armies had apparently made a mistake, one which, I am sure, no one in Bomber Command would ever have made. The generals had underestimated the enemy. That would always be an expensive error. Faced with the plum of Antwerp and its desirable port facilities, as well as the even greater prize of the Ruhr industrial complex, they had decided to go for both. As they reached out, they had been whacked severely on both wrists.

In the Ruhr sector, the debacle at Arnhem proved they had gone "a bridge too far". At the same time, the colossal task of opening the approaches to Antwerp harbour was left mainly to the Canadian 1st Army alone, under the very able leadership of General Crerar. It was an impossible task.

At a later date, and to his credit, Field Marshal Montgomery was to set forth a declaration in one of his books, an assertion that could have been made only by a big man: "I must admit a bad mistake on my part — I underestimated the difficulties of opening up the approaches to Antwerp so that we could get free use of the port. I reckoned that the Canadian Army could do this, while we were going for the Ruhr. I was wrong."

While the Allies faltered, the Germans consolidated all along the north-western front, making a veritable fortress of Walcheren Island which now dominated the sea channel entrance to the port of Antwerp. As the Canadian 1st Army, the Polish 1st Armoured Brigade, and the British 1st Corps lined up for a concerted attack on this Dutch front, they had no alternative but to call in the cavalry.

Bomber Command swept in over Walcheren Island, dropping leaflets telling the Dutch people what was about to happen. Twenty-four hours later the Lancasters and Mosquitos were back, this time with bombs. They cut the sea wall at Westkapelle, Veere, and both sides of Flushing. Despite the fact that the action had the approval of the Dutch Government in exile in London, it was taken hesitantly, reluctantly, and sadly. In addition to the number of German soldiers killed, many Dutch civilians also lost their lives. A million and a half precious young trees were destroyed.

280

The resultant flooding was necessary to flush out the enemy and facilitate the Allied advance, but it was utter disaster for the Dutch farmers and villagers in residence. Huge areas of fertile ground, most of it well below sea level, now lay under metres of corrosive, briny sea water. Land which had taken generations to win from the sea was surrendered back to this master in a few hours.

The old adage applied: "All's fair in love and war." This miserable platitude was of little help to the unfortunate Netherlanders, now left to wallow in the destructive waters and mud of this tactical manoeuvre. Though they quipped bravely at the time — "Better sea water than Germans" — the people in the area saw their crops ruined, grazing for the animals obliterated, their means of livelihood neutralised. The situation was grave.

Now those huge, mysterious panniers in Stores Section could come into play. Strung along the gaping bomb bay of each Lancaster, the carriers held a load of 7,000 pounds of food. There were sacks of flour, oatmeal, and sugar, huge commercial-size tins of fruit, vegetables and beans, together with tea, coffee, fresh vegetables, and mouth-watering, three-inch-thick, foot-long blocks of manufacturers' chocolate. In essence, there was everything to keep these unfortunate people alive until normality could come trickling slowly back to these vulnerable lowlands of Holland.

There was a great feeling of sympathy and consolation about these flights of mercy, all made in the name of Operation Manna. They may have started off tinged with high adventure as the scores of Lancasters roared out over the North Sea at 1,500 feet, easing down to 500 feet for the final run-in, but the mood changed markedly as the drop got underway, as the crews watched the scenes unfolding just outside their windscreens.

Men and women — some old, some young, some crippled, some down on their hands and knees — were scrambling to retrieve the commodities being dumped across the few remaining high points of their limited territory. We saw people wave, while others stumbled and fell as they moved over the rough ground. It would have been a hard man indeed who would not have been touched by the emotional scenes taking place not too far below the bombers.

I can assure you, without reservation, that I had one hell of a job trying to blink back the tears as I watched one old lady, already down on her knees, hands clasped together and held upwards, face staring towards the sky. Whether she was thanking her Maker, the Lancasters, or both, I will never know. At 150 knots and low-level flight, her's was an image that lasted but a fleeting moment in time for me, a moment that was to be etched deep for the rest of my life.

Yes, we would remember Operation Manna. Coming along after the deadly, dangerous business of delivering havoc and ruination from 20,000 feet, the "Spam" runs over Holland, as they were affectionately tagged, were an extremely pleasant way to spend an afternoon. Ironically, while my little old lady, her friends, and the crews in the Lancasters taking part will remember 8

May 1945 for Manna, the record books will tell the world that it was VE Day, the official date on which the Allies celebrated victory in Europe. Such trivia as "Spam" runs would quickly melt into the undergrowth of history, lost in the glare of newsreel scenes of tens of thousands of people, arms linked, singing and cheering their way across London's Trafalgar Square.

But then, distressful as these scenes in Holland may have been, other equally traumatic events were lurking just around the corner, waiting quietly to devastate and scar their way across our youthful arrogance.

The change from war to peace was quite a transformation. One day our leaders had this ambitious bombing campaign on their hands, manipulating hundreds of crews and four-engine bombers from bases all over the land. On the next and first day of peace, still with these crews and bombers, what were they to do with them? The main reason for their existence had gone, outdated by the unconditional surrender of the enemy. They didn't have long to wonder. Soon, calls for air services were coming in from interesting places.

First it was Manna, and now we were briefed for Operation Exodus. Hundreds of thousands of Allied prisoners of war were suddenly cut loose from camps all over the Reich, their repatriation given pinnacle priority, superseding almost every other call for movement.

Shipping could cope with vast numbers, but the luxury of potential enjoyed by our organisation was too good to ignore. Groups 1, 3, 4, 5, 6 and 8 of Bomber

283

Command had an almost limitless supply of aircraft and crews to call upon; ideal magic carpets to whisk the ex-PoWs back to freedom in a hurry.

Juvincourt was the contact airfield in France for our crew, a frontline base that had seen the conflict sway every which way since the outbreak of hostilities. Held in turn by French, German, and then Allied owners, this airfield had been bombed and strafed by all sides. When we got there in 1945, the ground and runways had been shot up, hacked up and refilled so many times that mesh steel grids had to be introduced. These carpets of metal squares were laid out end to end to form a makeshift runway of web steel over the rough ground. They helped to smooth things out quite a bit. Unfortunately, they were prone to edge up now and again, punching holes in Lancaster tyres as they did so. If this happened while we were shooting over them at speed, it could be embarrassing.

Our standard load was twenty-four ex-prisoners of war, they having been trucked through France from their stalags in Germany. We made many of these flights, but it was during the first one that we were taught a most salatory lesson.

As the current "Lords of the Air", never having experienced the trauma of a prisoner-of-war camp, we were revelling in our we'll-get-you-home act, oblivious — ignorant might be a better word — of the depth of the drama. Some of these men had been four, five, and even six years in enemy stalags. While there, they had no solid proof of the success or failure of the Allied effort. All they could do was to wait and hope and continue to suffer the humiliation of prison life under the Germans. To find themselves now climbing aboard an aircraft, the reality of their homeland just half an hour away, must have been truly unbelievable.

The sun was shining during that first Exodus touchdown. At Westcott Airfield in Buckinghamshire, wide expanses of lovely green grass stretched into the distance on either side of the wide acres of concrete.

To complete the picture, the Lancasters were lined up in a most impressive rank along one side of the area. To us, the crew, it was just another flight, so we helped the soldiers down from the plane, hanging around, possibly to chat. That was our big mistake.

To many of these people, this was an overwhelming emotional experience. Some got down on their hands and knees and kissed the concrete; some kissed the grass; others simply burst into tears where they stood; while yet others lay on the grass and sobbed. I was thunderstruck — acutely embarrassed — to say nothing of being near tears myself. Most of all, I was mortified that we had not anticipated these extreme emotions.

The Manna runs to Holland had been traumatic, but this was the ultimate emotional confrontation, eyeball to eyeball. We had well and truly blundered. By staying near the plane, we were impinging on privacies we had absolutely no right to share. These were our passengers' personal moments; their time, their experience. That was the important lesson we learned.

On all future Exodus trips, the boys and I simply left the plane and walked away, and never, ever looked

285

back. The right to take part in the scenes behind us had to be earned. We were merely the taxi drivers.

As group after group of these ex-prisoners of war, British and Indian, filed aboard our aircraft I would sometimes venture a glance, a nod, a smile. I've often wondered about the stories that lay behind the eyes, the docile manner, the resigned, rather sad, expression that would come back at me from these men; stories which, in the majority of cases, would possibly never be told in full. Happily, while they were in our charge, these servicemen assured two very important improvements. One, the discipline in my flying came back for a short time, much closer to the rule book; and two, our language and cross-talk on the RT, and in the plane in general, could be said to have become almost acceptable again.

In these free and easy early days of peace, the rules of the air were open to wide and wild interpretation. We would just fool around in general — low flying over the English Channel, playing tag with the ships — aware that the chance to jack around the skies like this would never come again.

Often during these junkets I would hear Harry belting out his repertoire of popular songs, most of them delivered in their rewrite versions. One of his favourites was the twisted translation of the ever popular *Stormy Weather*.

> "Don't know why
> Got no buttons on my fly
> Got a zipper

> Me and the girl think it's quicker
> We're on the job all the time."

Dear oh dear! There must have been people, somewhere, sitting up all night furiously rewriting the lyrics to most of the well-known musical ballads of the day. Usually the words got funnier, and the implications more involved as the verses rolled on. Maybe the authors figured that the acclaim Rupert Brooke had received for his poems during World War One, they could achieve in Rumble Number Two.

But then, in the middle of each Exodus run from France to the drop point for the ex-PoWs in England, the scene changed dramatically.

While our guests were aboard, everyone was on his best behaviour. My flying was as smooth as I could make it, and the landings were greased onto the runway. There were no old-fashioned take-offs at such times, where I'd keep the Lancaster roaring just a few feet above the runway, long after the wheels had been retracted, the kicker being to shoot up like an express lift at the tail end of the concrete. With twenty-four sensitive stomachs sitting in the body of the bomber, even the turns were slow and easy. We had watched our passengers come on board, each one clutching his little bag of glucose sweets, together with one other bag, just in case he was sick. These men were placing their trust in us, and we had no intention of breaking such a confidence.

I'm sure every pilot, every crew, if asked, would testify that it was a privilege to have been allowed to take part in Operation Exodus.

★ ★ ★

The French coastline was now sliding by below our wings. The Exodus runs had been replaced with Baedaker trips, five- to six-hour swings across Germany at a mere 1,500 feet. The idea was to take five or seven non-aircrew on a sightseeing run, allowing them to have a look at the acres of devastation, the end product of years of war. The Ruhr was the most sobering spectacle. Every bridge over the Rhine, as it snaked through Cologne, was dipping into the water, the remainder of the city an equally sorry sight.

Krupp's armament factories at Essen stretched on for miles, appearing as little more than huge piles of twisted steel and broken concrete. As city after city passed by our windows, the enormity of the destruction became cruelly clear. This time, retribution had really punched the Fatherland full of holes. This time, Germany itself had paid a truly terrible price for deciding to wage another war. At long weary last, we had to wonder if — maybe this time — the message had penetrated.

Their cruel, sadistic, all-conquering thousand-year Reich had lasted exactly twelve blistering years.

Next in line for the odd-job men came Operation Post Mortem, an escapade to test the efficiency of captured German radar.

Finally, we were switched to the disposal business. It seems our leaders had huge stocks of incendiary sticks, and like ourselves, these bombs had run out of targets and a war in which to manoeuvre. The deadly little inflammable missiles with their fire storms had reduced large tracts of such cities as Hamburg and Dresden to rubble. Now these demonic weapons were to be dumped unceremoniously into the watery wastes of the North Sea. With two flights per day, and bombed-up with ten 750-pound canisters of incendiary sticks, our Lancasters were pointed toward the north and given a predetermined Gee-H radar map reference to use as a dropping point.

Our crew, along with several others, had been moved from Stradishall to Mildenhall to take part in the disposal of these incendiary bombs. The memory of Stradishall, and the many happenings, tragedies and histrionics occurring there, would stay with us for the remainder of our lives.

The final curtain, though, was just around the corner. On 21 September 1945, the seven members of the Clueless Crew walked off in seven different directions, loners once again. For fourteen months we had been locked together in some of the hairiest exploits imaginable, flying up to and through the gates of Hell time and time again, relying explicitly on the skills and courage of one another. It needed only one link in the chain to buckle under pressure and we would have been sent spiralling and nose-diving into the obscurity of eternity way before our time. Each link held firm, and Lady Luck stayed with us. It was the sort of association and sharing of *esprit de corps* that very few people are privileged to experience. It was the sort of adventure that welded our friendships together for all time.

For me personally, my triad goal had been achieved. I had earned my pilot's Wings, had been posted to an operational squadron, and had measured up to the challenge of battle. The icing on the cake had been all of those beautiful people, interesting places, and high drama along the way.

I consider it an honour indeed to have served alongside the brave men in our crew, men who had gladly, almost casually, put their lives on the line. Shielded in the beautiful armour of *esprit de corps*, the seven of us had faced the ultimate enemy and been granted the privilege of walking away.

Our Maker had glanced in our direction, and smiled.

Epilogue

The Crew

Gerald Merrick [Navigator] was an accountant with a wholesale fruit organisation in Liverpool before joining the Royal Air Force in 1943. He returned to that profession following his demobilisation, retiring in 1980 to his home town of Maghull. Gerry never married. He lived alone until his death on Sunday, 7 August 1988. Our Navigator admitted to me that he never did see any of our targets, being too busy with his navigation charts, logs, and plans to take us back to base. Preferring night targets as opposed to daylight attacks, he was, in my opinion, by far the most important member of the crew — and that includes the pilot.

Harry Jenkinson [Wireless Operator] had always been fascinated by radio and its allied equipment. A youth at the outbreak of hostilities, he became involved with servicing and selling electronic supplies in the post-war years. Sadly, Harry died of a heart attack in 1970 while still comparatively young. Like Gerry, he never married, residing somewhere in London all his life. If there is a Valhalla, I just know that Harry will be walking wide across its courtyards, his great beaming smile spreading sunshine wherever he goes.

Jack Marner [Air Bomber] was also a Londoner, employed both pre- and post-war with the Wellcome Pharmaceutical Company. When we formed as a crew originally, he was the only one of the seven to hold the King's commission. Like many aircrew members, Jack started his flying career as a trainee pilot, but was regraded as air bomber while in Canada. I am sure he would have made a very good pilot, but he was caught up in a system that found itself with far too many "drivers" already. Married during the war, Jack retired from his civilian job early because of health problems. He now resides in Westmoors, Dorset. Sadly, Jack lost his beautiful wife, Sadie, in 1986. He, too, preferred riding bombers in the dark. As he said, it was a question of, "I can't see them; they can't see me". Like me, Jack loathed those lingering black plumes left behind by flak that had exploded and gone on its nefarious way.

Frank Parkhouse [Flight Engineer] was 42 years of age when he joined the crew, making him the daddy of the group. An engineer in civilian life, he was a natural for Flight Engineer with us. Frank died at age 50, just eight years after returning to his civilian career. He, like Ivor, was from Devon, a county in which he resided all of his peacetime life. It has always puzzled me why, at the age of 42, our Engineer would want to dice with death over enemy targets.

Ivor "Blondie" Foster [Mid-upper Gunner] has always had his home in and around Plymouth, Devon, where he resides to this day. I visited Ivor and his wife, Bernice, in 1994. They have two sons, both of whom are now married. Ivor joined the Devonshire Police Force when released from his Service career, and attained the rank of sergeant. Bernice and Ivor assisted at a school for the mentally challenged until quite recently, Bernice retiring in 1989, and Ivor in 1993. Blondie (as Ivor was known to his crew) had two aversions. He objected strongly to other bombers poised flush above us with their bomb doors already open, and, secondly, he had a thing about searchlights. They ruined his night vision. Indeed, he had no love for night targets.

Clinton "Clin" Booth [Rear Gunner] originated from the pottery area around Stoke-on-Trent. After leaving the Royal Air Force in 1946, Clin returned to that region and became a sales representative with one of the potteries. He, too, married at the end of hostilities. Clin and his wife, Betty, lived in the little township of Biddulph, Staffordshire. Betty had been a member of the Women's Auxiliary Air Force. One of their great joys was the care of their beautiful gardens, the serenity of which was a far cry from the hell of the skies over wartime Gelsenkirchen. Sadly, again, Clin died in October 1993.

Philip Gray [Pilot]. At the outbreak of hostilities I was a student at Bruce's Business College, Dundee, becoming a temporary civil servant with the Ministry of Food one year later. Returning from war duties, I opened my own retail business, and married my lovely wife, Lynn, in 1952. During 1953/54 I returned to active flying duties, assigned to the 2nd Tactical Air Force in Germany, where I served as a tow pilot on the four firing ranges off the coast of the Island of Sylt, north Germany. We used the Tempest, Mosquito and Meteor as tow planes. Later I acquired a private pilot's licence which I maintained until 1989. My wife and I emigrated to New Zealand in 1971 where, sadly, I lost her in 1982. In 1991 I moved to Toronto, Canada.

Glossary

Aldis Lamp	A hand-held piece of equipment used for sending messages from point to point. The lamp consists of a large, round glass face powered from an electric or battery source. A set of pivotal slats blanket off the light beam, the light being exposed only when the slats are turned on their axis through 90°. The operator exposes a longer or shorter beam to signify a dot or a dash of the Morse code.
Ack-Ack or Flak	Anti-aircraft gunfire.
Angels	Height, e.g. Angels Ten = 10,000 feet.
Biscuits	Three small biscuit-shaped mattresses which, when placed end to end, become one person-sized mattress.
BFTS	British Flying Training School.
Chop	
Chopper	
Bought it	
Hammer	} Killed
Axed	
Iced	
Past-tensed	

Cookie	} 4,000-pound bomb.
Blockbuster	
DROs	Daily Routine Orders.
Doodlebug	Slang name for the V-1 missile — the first of the unmanned aerial explosive devices used by the Germans, and dispatched over Britain toward the end of World War Two.
ETW	Elementary Training Wing.
EFTS	Elementary Flying Training School.
FFI	Free From Infection — a medical examination for all trainees to ensure that they were free from any contracted disease such as venereal disease.
Fingers, The	V-sign given with the index and middle fingers — a derogatory gesture.
Fizzer	To be put on a charge; to be charged with a misdemeanour.
Flaming Onions	Light calibre anti-aircraft shells; so called because they would arc up from the ground as a string of beautiful coloured balls of fire. The colours, I presume, would represent the different types of shells — anti-personnel, incendiary, armour piercing, etc.

FIDO	Fog Investigation and Dispersal Operation.
Gen or Griff	Information.
Gee	Radar equipment which, when used in coordination with special maps, can pinpoint the exact position of the aircraft.
Gee-H	Similar to Gee, only this type of radar uses mobile stations to send out its radio signals. During World War Two, these stations could (and did) move forward with the front line and so provide accurate pinpointing for bombers zeroing in on enemy targets.
GR	General Reconnaissance.
Heat Wagon	Fire Tender.
H2S	Airborne radar equipment which can present a map-type picture on the cathode ray tube screen.
Happy Valley	The Ruhr Valley industrial area of Germany.
ITW	Initial Training Wing.
Irons	Service jargon for the all-metal issue cutlery set of fork, knife and spoon.
Kite	Aeroplane.
Losing your ring	A vulgar expression meaning "to be sick".

Last Three	The last three numerals of a service person's official service number. A person's name and last three were used as a means of identification in each situation where positive verification was vital, e.g. on Pay Parade.
Meat Wagon	Ambulance. Another popular name for this vehicle was "blood wagon".
PFF	Pathfinder Force.
PR	Photographic Reconnaissance.
RT	Radio Telephony.
Screamers **The Screams**	} Diarrhoea.
Tannoy	The internal communication system of an airfield. The loud-speakers would be attached to trees and buildings all over the complex.
Three-Ringer	Wing Commander.
USAAC	United States Army Air Corps.
Verey Pistol	A gun which can be fired either from the ground or from an aircraft. It issues brightly coloured identification balls of flaming material.
V-2	The second and much more powerful unmanned aerial explosive device sent toward Britain by the Germans. While the V-1 flew at a low level just like a conventional aircraft, the V-2 reached heights of

	60,000 to 65,000 feet before plummeting back to earth. There was no sure method to aim these devices accurately at specific targets, so they simply landed and exploded quite indiscriminately. They were pointed in the general direction of London.
VHF	Very High Frequency.
Wimpy	Term used for the Wellington aircraft.
Wanganui flares	Target markers or identification flares used by the Pathfinder unit over enemy targets.
Washed-out	Failed or removed from a training course.

Appendix

The Lancaster: Engines And Equipment

There were three Marks of this heavy bomber, namely I, III and X. The Mark I had de Havilland three-blade hydromatic propellers but, while this Mark was fitted with Merlin 20, 22 or 24 engines, Mark III had Merlin 28 or 38 engines. The Lancaster Mark X was built in Canada and differed from the British bombers in some of the instruments and in the electrical systems.

Three self-sealing fuel tanks were fitted into each wing, the fuel carried in either side being 1,077 Imperial gallons, a total of 2,154 gallons. If necessary, two extra tanks, each with a capacity of 400 gallons, could be fitted into the bomb cells. Each Rolls-Royce Merlin engine had its own oil tank of 37½ gallons.

The main services were provided by hydraulic, pneumatic and electrical systems.

The hydraulics, operating through an individual engine-driven pump for each gun turret, were linked up as follows: the pump on the starboard outer engine serviced the mid-upper turret; that on the starboard inner engine serviced the front turret; the port inner engine controlled the mid-under gun turret; while the port outer engine serviced the tail turret.

Not all Lancasters had provision for a mid-under gun turret. If fitted, it usually housed a 0.5 calibre gun. The hydraulics also operated the undercarriage, flaps, bomb doors, carburettor air intake shutters, and fuel jettisoning.

The pneumatic system was maintained by two compressors and two vacuum pumps. The Heywood compressor on the starboard inner engine operated the wheel brakes, radiator shutters, supercharger rams, and idle cut-off rams for each engine. An RAE compressor on the port inner operated the automatic controls and the computer for the Mark XIV bombsight. A vacuum pump is fitted into each inboard engine, one for operating the instruments on the pilot's flying panel, and the other for operating the gyros of the Mark XIV bombsight.

Finally, the electrical system had its power supplied by two 1,500-watt generators, one on each inboard engine. These generators would charge the aircraft batteries (24 volt) and supply the usual lighting, together with such services as propeller feathering pumps, flap and undercarriage indicators, pressure head heating, fuel booster pumps, radio equipment, landing lamps, engine starting and booster coils, dinghy inflation, controls for radiator, supercharger and cutoff rams, bomb gear and bombsight, engine fire extinguishers, fuel contents gauges, fuel pressure warning lights and gauges, the camera, heated clothing, and the DR (Dead Reckoning) compass.

Maximum speeds in miles per hour

Diving	360
Bomb doors open	360
Undercarriage down	200
Flaps down	200
Straight & level	275

Maximum weights

Take-off and straight flying	65,000lb
Landing & all manoeuvre flying	55,000lb
Flying should be restricted to straight & level until weight is reduced to	63,000lb

Maximum performance when climbing

160mph to 12,000 feet
155mph from 12,000 to 18,000 feet
150mph from 18,000 to 22,000 feet
145mph above 22,000 feet

Maximum range 2,700 miles (4,345 km)

Maximum load   22,000lb

First entered service 24 December 1941

Total number Lancasters built 7,377

Then again, if the opposition should get lucky, there were a wide range of interesting devices and procedures available in and around a Lancaster bomber for the use of the crew. Some of these are listed below.

302

Fire

If there was a fire in the bomb bay caused by enemy action, then the bay doors would be opened, the bombs jettisoned, and the plane put into a dive. If, even after this action, the fire continued to spread, the crew would abandon the aircraft.

Bomb Jettisoning

If, for one reason or another, the bomb load became an embarrassment and had to be jettisoned, the bomb doors were opened and a check made visually through the peep hole to ensure that both doors were open. The 500-pound bombs and the incendiary clusters were always dumped first, followed by the 4,000-pound blockbuster. It was lethal to drop the big bomb first because of the grave danger of the 500-pounders colliding with it, the resulting explosion then destroying the plane. When all bombs had been jettisoned, the bomb doors were closed.

Parachute Exits

The hatch in the floor of the bomb aimer's compartment was to be used by all members of the crew. This escape opening was in the nose of the aircraft, the door being opened by a twist of the handle. The door was lifted inwards, and then jettisoned through the hatch opening. The main entrance/exit door at the rear of the fuselage would be used as a last resort. Those using this rear door to exit with a parachute would take great care, diving out through the lower part of the doorway, head first. This action saved heads from being bounced off the tail unit by the back draft.

Crash Exits

Once a Lancaster had hit the deck, the crew was to abandon the aircraft as quickly as possible. Use could be made of the three pushout panels built into the roof of the fuselage.

Dinghy

A large dinghy was stored in the starboard wing of a Lancaster, and was released by:

(a) pulling a release cord which ran along the roof at the rear of the fuselage inside the bomber

(b) pulling the release loop on the outside located on the leading edge of the starboard side of the tail plane's horizontal unit, or

(c) pushing an immersion switch, which activated automatically when it hit the water.

Fire Extinguishers

Each engine had its own built-in extinguisher. These could be activated by push buttons on the pilot's instrument panel or automatically by a crash switch. There were five hand-held fire extinguishers inside the bomber.

Incendiary Bombs

Two of these were strapped on to the front face of the front spar inside the Lancaster. These were to be used to destroy the bomber if it crashed inside enemy territory.

The last major mission flown by Lancasters of Bomber Command during World War Two is reported to have taken place on 25 April 1945, when 318 aircraft bombed Hitler's mountain residence at Berchtesgaden. On the night of 2 May 1945, the Royal Air Force flew its last operational raid on Germany when Mosquitos of the Light Night Striking Force raided and successfully bombed Kiel Harbour. On 7 May 1945, General Jodl of the German High Command signed the joint surrender of the German Armed Forces, to become effective at 1201 hours on 9 May 1945.

Number 186 Squadron

This Squadron was attached to 3 Group and was assigned the code letters XY/AP. 186 was re-formed at Tuddenham on 5 October 1944 as a two-flight squadron by the transfer of an initial ten Lancasters from "C" Flight, Number 90 Squadron. Two nights later twelve Lancasters were available for the Squadron's first operation — an attack on Bonn. A move to Stradishall was made the following mid-December. Until the end of the war the Squadron operated Mark I Lancasters almost exclusively.

Also available in ISIS Large Print:

In the Face of the Enemy

Ernest Powdrill, MC

"Suddenly a hail of machine-gun bullets were fired in our direction, with one or two ripping into the canvas roof of my tractor a couple of feet from my head. I was standing up at the time with both hands gripping the top of the windscreen."

In the Face of the Enemy is a no-holds-barred account of the author's experiences in an artillery regiment with the British Expeditionary Force in 1939 and 1940 and, four years later, in North West Europe closing in on Nazi Germany.

Ernest Powdrill joined the Territorials in 1935 and transferred to the Regular Army in 1938. By the time his regiment went out to France in September 1939 he was a full sergeant in command of a 25-pounder Mark 1 gun.

ISBN 978-0-7531-9534-5 (hb)
ISBN 978-0-7531-9535-2 (pb)

Escaper's Progress

David James

"Never had I foreseen that the enemy's fire would be so literally like a curtain; a safety curtain to him, since for us to fire torpedoes with any hope of success we had to see the target."

David James was serving in Motor Gun Boats when he was captured in February 1943. Imprisoned initially in Dulag Marlag, he immediately decided to escape. His first tunnel was discovered before completion. In December 1943 he succeeded in escaping and was on the run for almost a week disguised as an officer of the Royal Bulgarian Navy. He was captured while attempting to board a ship at Lubeck.

Undeterred, in February 1944 he broke out again, this time dressed as a Swedish sailor. Travelling by train to Bremen, Hamburg, Lubeck, Rostock and Danzig, he eventually succeeded in reaching Stockholm after two and a half days in a ship's engine room.

ISBN 978-0-7531-8380-9 (hb)
ISBN 978-0-7531-8381-6 (pb)

Night Action

Peter Dickens

"When I poked my head out of the window, his head was out further along the carriage. He smiled at me and twiddled a revolver around his finger."

In all the annals of the war at sea, comparatively little has been written about the role of the torpedo boat, and yet these small boats were at the heart of some of the most dangerous actions of the War. Travelling at high speed and amid storms and gunfire, and usually under the cover of darkness, these vulnerable craft sought out enemy convoys and escorts and wrought havoc among the German supply lines.

Night Action is Peter Dickens' account of his experiences as the young commander of the 21st MTB Flotilla during 1942-43. Lively and thrilling, while there is humour to be found, the horror of war is never far away.

ISBN 978-0-7531-8382-3 (hb)
ISBN 978-0-7531-8383-0 (pb)

RAF Liberator Over the Eastern Front

Jim Auton

"At our age, nobody would have allowed us to drive a car, borrow a motorbike or vote, but the Royal Air Force offered us the chance to leave home and fly an aeroplane. So we were hooked."

In 1941, Jim Auton enlisted in the wartime RAF as a pupil pilot. On learning that Air Bombers, a new category of aircrew, were serving as bomb aimers and co-pilots he opted for that role instead. Eventually he arrived in the south Italian war zone, flying B24 Liberators over dangerous targets such as Munich. Jim was severely wounded, and his flying career ended when he was only 20.

After the war, Jim set up a number of successful businesses with contacts in Communist controlled countries. This brought him to the attention of the Secret Services. He was ordered to become a spy but refused, with dire consequences. In his memoirs, Jim shares some of his most exciting ventures.

ISBN 978-0-7531-9520-8 (hb)
ISBN 978-0-7531-9521-5 (pb)

Mosquito Victory

Jack Currie

"I levelled the Mosquito out at twenty-thousand feet, and gently tipped the right wing down. The lumps and hollows of the Cotswolds swung slowly round the long, smooth cowling of the starboard Merlin."

Jack Currie graphically describes the life of a wartime RAF bomber pilot on "rest", first instructing trainees on the four-engined Halifax bomber then later training as a glider pilot. He returned to operations with the Pathfinder force flying Mosquitoes of the 1409 Weather Flight. He was awarded the DFC in 1944, and was flying Mosquitoes when the war in Europe ended.

ISBN 978-0-7531-9516-1 (hb)
ISBN 978-0-7531-9517-8 (pb)

ISIS publish a wide range of books in large print, from fiction to biography. Any suggestions for books you would like to see in large print or audio are always welcome. Please send to the Editorial Department at:

ISIS Publishing Limited
7 Centremead
Osney Mead
Oxford OX2 0ES

A full list of titles is available free of charge from:

Ulverscroft Large Print Books Limited

(UK)
The Green
Bradgate Road, Anstey
Leicester LE7 7FU
Tel: (0116) 236 4325

(Australia)
P.O. Box 314
St Leonards
NSW 1590
Tel: (02) 9436 2622

(USA)
P.O. Box 1230
West Seneca
N.Y. 14224-1230
Tel: (716) 674 4270

(Canada)
P.O. Box 80038
Burlington
Ontario L7L 6B1
Tel: (905) 637 8734

(New Zealand)
P.O. Box 456
Feilding
Tel: (06) 323 6828

Details of **ISIS** complete and unabridged audio books are also available from these offices. Alternatively, contact your local library for details of their collection of **ISIS** large print and unabridged audio books.